Elie Wiesel

Titles in the **Holocaust Heroes and Nazi Criminals** *series:*

Adolf Eichmann
Executing the "Final Solution"
0-7660-2575-6

Adolf Hitler
Evil Mastermind of the Holocaust
0-7660-2533-0

Anne Frank
Hope in the Shadows of the Holocaust
0-7660-2531-4

Elie Wiesel
Surviving the Holocaust, Speaking Out Against Genocide
0-7660-2576-4

Heinrich Himmler
Murderous Architect of the Holocaust
0-7660-2532-2

Oskar Schindler
Saving Jews From the Holocaust
0-7660-2534-9

Raoul Wallenberg
Rescuing Thousands From the Nazis' Grasp
0-7660-2530-6

Holocaust Heroes and Nazi Criminals

Elie Wiesel

Surviving the Holocaust, Speaking Out Against Genocide

Lisa Moore

Enslow Publishers, Inc.

40 Industrial Road   PO Box 38
Box 398   Aldershot
Berkeley Heights, NJ 07922   Hants GU12 6BP
USA   UK

http://www.enslow.com

Dedicated to Lawrence Abraham Margolin (1913–1979)

Acknowledgments

Thank you to: Dr. John MacDonald, University of Notre Dame, 1976, for introducing me to Elie Wiesel; Helen Strahinich for recommending me for this project and for her support as editor and mentor; the Howard Gotlieb Archival Research Center at Boston University; Cate Hunter at The School of Theology at Boston University; Maren L. Read, Photo Archives, United States Holocaust Memorial Museum; Ann Siekman and the Norway Public Library; Ken Morse and Grassroots Graphics; Thomas Victor and his sister, Harriet Spurlin, for the use of their photographs; three readers: Lance Deschenes, Helen Strahinich, & Maggie Mayer; an assistant, Chelsea Peterson; my editor at Enslow Publishers; Lee and Sam Margolin for compensating during a winter of research and obsession; and, of course, to Eliezer ben Shlomo Wiesel.

Library of Congress Cataloging-in-Publication Data:

Moore, Lisa, 1955–
    Elie Wiesel: surviving the Holocaust, speaking out against genocide / Lisa Moore.
       p. cm. — (Holocaust heroes and Nazi criminals)
    Includes bibliographical references and index.
    ISBN-10: 0-7660-2576-4
      1. Wiesel, Elie, 1928– —Juvenile literature. 2. Jews—Romania—Sighet—Biography—
Juvenile literature. 3. Concentration camp inmates—Biography—Juvenile literature.
4. Holocaust, Jewish (1939–1945)—Juvenile literature. 5. Holocaust survivors—
Biography—Juvenile literature. 6. Jewish authors—Biography—Juvenile literature.
I. Title. II. Series.
    DS135.R73W545 2005
    940.53'18'092—dc22   2004030085

ISBN-13: 978-0-7660-2576-9

Printed in the United States of America

10 9 8 7 6 5 4 3 2

To Our Readers: We have done our best to make sure all Internet addresses in this book
were active and appropriate when we went to press. However, the author and the publisher
have no control over and assume no liability for the material available on those Internet
sites or on other Web sites they may link to. Any comments or suggestions can be sent by
e-mail to comments@enslow.com or to the address on the back cover.

Illustration Credits: Associated Press, AP, pp. 106, 108, 124; Clipart.com, p. 20; Courtesy of
Michael A. Schuman, p. 11; Courtesy of Thomas Victor, pp. 80, 86, 93, 135; Courtesy of
USHMM Photo Archives, pp. 7, 8, 9, 16, 28, 36, 49, 58, 63, 66, 68, 104, 127, 138 (top and
second from bottom), 139 (bottom), 141 (second from bottom), 143, 152, 154, 157, 158; Elie
Wiesel Archives at Boston University, pp. 95, 112; Harry Lore, courtesy of the USHMM
Photo Archives, p. 141 (top); James Sanders, courtesy of the USHMM Photo Archives, pp. 29,
139 (top); Lorenz Schmuhl, courtesy of the USHMM Photo Archives, pp. 138 (third from
bottom), 140 (top), 141 (third from bottom); The Main Commission for the Persecution of
the Crimes Against the Polish Nation, courtesy of USHMM Photo Archives, pp. 138 (second
from top), 140 (bottom), 141 (second from top); National Archives and Records
Administration, pp. 32, 42, 45, 51, 53, 60, 138 (third from top), 141 (third from top), 142;
The National Museum of American Jewish History, courtesy of USHMM Photo Archives,
pp. 138 (bottom), 141 (bottom); Reproduced from the Collections of the Library of Congress,
p. 31.

Cover Illustration: Courtesy of Michael A. Schuman

Contents

Fast Facts About Elie Wiesel

Name: Eliezer (Elie) Wiesel

Born: September 30, 1928 in Sighet, Romania

Family: Father—Shlomo Wiesel (died 1945); Mother—Sarah Feig (died 1944); Sister—Bea (1926–1974); Sister—Hilda (born 1922) lives in Nice, France; Wife—Marion Rose (married 1969); Son—Elisha Wiesel (born 1972)

Education: The Sorbonne, University of Paris, 1948–1951

Jobs held: Journalist for Israeli, French, and American newspapers; Over fifty books written and published, 1960–present; Chairman, United States President's Commission on the Holocaust, 1979–1980; Chairman, United States Holocaust Memorial Council,1980–1986; Boston University, Andrew W. Mellon Professor in Humanities, 1976–present

Notable for: *Night* (1960), world's most widely-read piece of Holocaust testimony; United States Congressional Gold Medal, 1985; Nobel Peace Prize, 1986; Elie and Marion Wiesel Foundation for Humanity, established 1986

1

The Return

> And yet. Those are my two favorite words, applicable to
> every situation, be it happy or bleak. The sun is rising?
> And yet it will set. A night of anguish? And yet it too,
> will pass.[1]

On an autumn day in 1964, thirty-six-year-old Elie Wiesel
traveled to Sighet, his hometown in Romania, to look for
something he had left behind.

He took a big plane from New York City to Europe. He
took a smaller plane to Bucharest, the capital of Romania. In
Bucharest, he boarded an even smaller plane for Baia Mare, to
the northwest.

In Baia Mare, Wiesel hired a taxi to cross the Carpathian
Mountains for about 120 miles. The roads were poorly lit,
bumpy and rough, and the car was an old Volga. Day melted
into night. The driver was not too interested in conversation,
but Wiesel did manage to get a few answers out of him.

"Do you know Sighet?" Wiesel asked the driver.

"Yes."

"What do you think of it?"

"Why, it's just a town, a town like any other."

"What does it look like?"

"There's nothing to tell."

"Are there still Jews living there?"

"Jews? I don't know any."[2]

The winding road finally began to descend from the dramatic Romanian peaks. The old car passed through quaint villages as colorful as candy. Small gardens were ready for the autumn harvest.

After six hours, the taxi driver announced they were getting close. Fifteen miles away, then five. Finally, they arrived. The whole trip had taken about three days . . . and twenty years. Although Elie Wiesel spent the first fifteen years of his life in Sighet, he had not returned since he left in the spring of 1944.

The taxi stopped in the middle of town. "Here we are," said the driver.

"Are you sure this is Sighet?" Wiesel asked. The driver said yes and got back into the car. He had to return to Baia Mare that night.

It was late and silent. Almost everyone in the town was asleep. Wiesel stood with his suitcase and looked around. He looked at the buildings, their roofs and their chimneys, and the black sky above. He crossed the cold street to the Hotel Corona, walking with a bit of a limp, still stiff from his long journey. He remembered the hotel as a luxurious palace, but on this night, it looked shabby, run down, and dimly lit. Things change in twenty years.

On the second floor, the night clerk sat bundled in a thick blanket. When Wiesel asked for a room, the clerk said that he

Elie Wiesel

could not have one without a reservation, even though there were vacancies. It was the rule, he explained. When Wiesel gave the clerk a tip, he was offered a room. The clerk took out a register and asked for his name and where he was from.

"New York," Wiesel answered.

The clerk was surprised. "You came from New York? To Sighet?" Not many people from far away visited Sighet. The clerk took Wiesel to his room.

But Wiesel did not sleep. Instead, he went back out into the night. He stood on the town square and took a deep breath. He had come here to find something, something he had left behind. Why wait any longer? Why not look for it now?

Strangely, he felt that he had returned here before, but it had not been real. He had imagined returning to Sighet in such detail that it *seemed* real. He had even written about it in one of his many books, *The Town Beyond the Wall.* Its main character, Michael, returned to his hometown—after the war—just like this.

He walked past the place where the fire station used to be. It was no longer there. Further on, the church. Oh yes, the church was still there, but he doubted that the synagogues were. He noticed a street sign. It had changed. What used to be the Jews' Street, was now the "Street of the Deported."

Suddenly Wiesel started running.

He ran as fast as he could in the direction of his old house. Finally, he stood in front of it. It looked smaller than he remembered it, more aged, more beaten by time and weather. But he remembered it all: the walls, the neighbors, the garden, his classmates. And the day they were forced to leave.

He ran his fingers over the fence that surrounded the house. He walked all around it. He touched the walls and the windows. The strangers inside continued to sleep, unaware of the strange prowler. His heart raced.

He grabbed the door handle of the backyard gate and turned it. It squeaked. He opened it just enough to slip inside. There he was in his yard, his family's yard. The barrel at the entrance to the cellar was still there. The same bucket still hung above the well. The same tree still stood in the garden, taller now. Its limbs were bare in the cold autumn night.

Here was the barn. There was the fence. He stood in the same spot he had been in April 1944. He remembered everything as if it were yesterday. Three steps that way. Two steps this way. He fell to his knees and touched the spot. He began to dig with his hands. The ground was hard and cold. His fingernails inched downward, his muscles straining with effort. Finally, his frozen fingers reached something metal. It was the box. It was still there after all these years.

Elie Wiesel gently took the box from its burial place. He was trembling, remembering what was inside. He pushed the top of the box and it opened. The watch was still there.

> Covered with dirt and rust, crawling with worms, it is unrecognizable, revolting. I am angry with myself for having yielded to curiosity, but disappointment gives way to profound pity: the watch too lived through war and holocaust, the kind reserved for watches perhaps. In its way, it too is a survivor, a ghost infested with humiliating sores and obsolete memories.[3]

When Elie Wiesel was thirteen, his parents gave him this watch for his *bar mitzvah*, the ceremony that celebrates a Jewish boy's passage into manhood. When the Germans came, his family buried their most precious possessions in the backyard, hoping that they would still be there when the war was over. His mother buried the two silver candlesticks that they used only on Fridays to celebrate the Sabbath. His father buried jewelry and papers. Young Elie Wiesel? He buried his bar mitzvah watch.

Wiesel sat there, in the darkness, in a stranger's backyard, staring and crying. The sky grew red in the east. He placed the watch back into its box and then placed the box back into the earth. He filled the hole with his hands and stood up. He wiped his face and went back through the gate. He closed it behind him as he left the yard.

As far as anyone knows, Elie Wiesel's watch is still there.[4]

Wiesel walked back through the empty streets of the town. That day, in a daze, he wandered around Sighet. He went to the hospital and the library. He wanted to see the synagogues again. There used to be fifty; now there was one. He spoke to few people, was remembered by no one, and finally, went to the Jewish cemetery. There, he visited his grandfather's grave, the man for whom he was named.

In the cemetery, Wiesel noticed a slanted block of stone with a few words engraved on it, a cold, unliving memorial for ten thousand Jews, none of whom were buried here. It held no names, but it held millions of memories. Wiesel lit a candle despite a strong wind.

Twenty-four hours after he arrived in Sighet, Wiesel left. It had been enough. Perhaps it had been too much. The town was no longer his. In fact, Sighet, as he knew it, no longer existed. Life, as he knew it then, no longer existed. Everything had changed.

Elie Wiesel survived the Holocaust, which was the mass murder of 11 million people, including 6 million Jews, by the Nazis during World War II. He authored over fifty books, taught at prestigious universities, received scores of honorary degrees, and influenced leaders all over the world. In 1986, he won the Nobel Prize for Peace, which is, in the minds of many, the greatest honor a human being can achieve. His miraculous life began here in Sighet, in 1928.

As Elie Wiesel rode the taxi out of town, he once again saw the main square, the movie theater, the pastry shop, the girls' high school, and the church steeple. He saw a policeman, a little girl holding her mother's arm, and a couple gazing into a store window. As the taxi turned a corner, he caught one last glimpse of his house before they wound their way back through the mountains that had sheltered his youth.[5]

2

Sighet

In the autumn of 1928, a family named Wiesel lived in Sighet, a village in the Carpathian Mountains in Romania. Sarah and Shlomo Wiesel already had two daughters named Hilda and Bea, ages six and two, and Sarah was expecting a third child soon. It was the end of the Jewish year, the time when Jews all over the world finish the yearly cycle of reading the Torah, the holy book. They read it one passage at a time when they gather together to worship.

The year ended on the twenty-third day of the month of Tishri on the Jewish calendar. In 1928, the twenty-third of Tishri fell on September 30. This day is a Jewish holiday called Simhat Torah (rejoicing in the Torah). For the Wiesel family, the day was doubly blessed. On that day, in their stone house on Serpent Street, a son was born. They praised the god of Abraham, Isaac, and Jacob and prayed that their son would live a long and blessed life.

Shlomo and Sarah named the baby after Shlomo's father, Eliezer, who served in the army of the Austro-Hungarian

Empire in World War I, back when Sighet was part of Hungary. Eliezer had carried wounded men on stretchers and was killed while he helped a fellow soldier. The Wiesels heard stories about him from his widow, Grandma Nissel, a pale, thin woman who always wore a black scarf.

Shlomo owned a grocery store in town and the whole family, including Grandma Nissel, stocked the shelves and waited on customers. Wiesel remembers his father as a "cultured, rather unsentimental man" who was "more concerned with others than with his own family."[1] To adults in Sighet, it seemed Shlomo was always willing to help people in trouble. His foremost concern was his community, especially the safety and protection of its Jews.

After the grocery store closed in the evening, Shlomo usually went to the local community offices where he volunteered to help Jews with immigration matters. In Europe in 1930, many people were moving from country to country, especially Jews. Communities of European Jews have always moved around a lot, often not by their own choice. In fact, Sighet was a shtetl, a small Jewish village, founded three hundred years earlier by Jews who were driven out of Russia. In 1930, its population was about twenty-five thousand. Well over half—about fifteen thousand—were Jews.

The Jewish Faith

To understand Elie Wiesel, it is essential to know something about Judaism, one of the world's major religions, practiced by people who call themselves Jews. Jews are a group of people who believe they are descended from Abraham, Isaac, and Jacob in the land of Canaan thirty-seven hundred years ago. You do not have to be born Jewish, however, to be Jewish. Anyone who is willing to assume the obligation of the practice and commandments of Judaism can become a Jew.

Everything in the Wiesels' life—family, friends, and community—was centered on the traditions and beliefs of Judaism. Their food, their language, their holidays, what the children learned in school—Jewish laws and customs ruled it all. Judaism was a religion, a culture, and a heritage. It was also both present and past; Jewish roots extended back thousands of years. Stories of Jewish history were handed down from generation to generation in vivid detail. Sometimes, to Elie, the stories seemed more real than real life, the way movies are for some people today.

Hebrew is the ancient language of the Jews. Elie learned it at an early age but did not speak it with his family and friends. At home and in the neighborhood, the Wiesels spoke Yiddish, the language of Jews all over Europe. All the stories and songs and gossip and jokes were in Yiddish, a symphony of Hebrew, Russian, Polish, English, and German. The Wiesels also understood enough Hungarian, German, Romanian, Ruthenian, Ukrainian, and Russian to be able to speak with their non-Jewish customers.[2]

How can you tell if someone is Jewish? You cannot. By law, in Germany in 1935, however, you were Jewish if two to four of your grandparents were Jewish. You were also Jewish if you belonged to a Jewish religious community on or after September 15, 1935.[3] These two criteria described about 9.5 million European Jews when Elie Wiesel was a child. Jews lived all over Europe, but mostly in Eastern Europe; there was hardly a town without a Jewish community. In Poland, 10 percent of the population, more than 3 million people, were Jewish.[4]

Two thousand years ago, in the earliest days of Christianity, Christians often tried to convert everyone else, but many people, including many Jews, refused to give up their faith. As a result, certain zealous Christian church leaders resorted to violence. In the cities, they crowded Jews into small areas called ghettos. During the Middle Ages (400 to 1450 A.D.), militant Christians expelled Jews from countries and destroyed their villages. They burned Jewish books and, sometimes, Jews themselves.

From the eleventh through the nineteenth centuries, Christian governments throughout Europe passed laws to limit Jewish rights. Jews could not attend universities, hold public offices, or own property. Jews could not marry Christians, eat with them, or work with them. Jews were blamed for poisoning wells, causing diseases, and killing Jesus.[5] If someone was murdered, a Jew was blamed. If the economy went bad, it must be the fault of the Jews.

By the beginning of the twentieth century, however, Jews had nearly the same rights in Europe as others. In many places, especially in cities, they were accepted as equals. Jews were among Europe's most respected writers, poets, doctors, and scientists.[6] But underneath this public acceptance, another wave of anti-Semitism sprouted in the narrow minds of many working-class Europeans who were impoverished by a demolished economy after World War I. This prejudice against the Jews of Europe grew like a wild vine.

Jews were the targets of discriminatory laws and violent outbursts. Between 1920 and 1930, laws limiting the rights of Jews were passed in Poland, Latvia, Romania, Lithuania, and Greece. In some places, Jews could not use telephones, radios, or public transportation. In Germany in 1922, a Jewish government leader named Walther Rathenau was murdered by people who directed anti-Semitic slogans at him. A new movement against the Jews was under way.

Jewish children learned to be wary of Christians. Wiesel recalls that sometimes, on Christmas Eve, Christian boys

wearing masks and horns carried whips into the streets at night, pretending to hunt for Jews, the people who they claimed killed Jesus.[7] It was a childish game rooted in hatred and fear. In an interview in 1982, Wiesel said, "As a child, I took it as a law of nature to be hated by the non-Jew. It was clear to me that if I went on the street, sooner or later I would be beaten up."[8]

Family, Friends, and Freedom

Elie grew up thinking his family was wealthy. Relative to many, it was. The Wiesel children got treats . . . but not often and never too many. "When we bought cherries, we got ten each. When there was corn, it was one ear per person. Three apricots or a piece of watermelon or cantaloupe on a summer's evening was a rare treat."[9]

Today, Wiesel admits that he secretly wished he were poor. His hungry classmates made him feel guilty, and he felt he would be more devout if his life were more miserable. He often gave away his food and even admits giving away money that his family sorely needed.[10]

By his own admission, Wiesel was sickly and shy. "I complained easily. . . . I spent too much time daydreaming with my friends instead of studying. I didn't eat enough and my parents worried constantly about how thin I was, and how pale. Lavish sums were spent dragging me from doctor to doctor, city to city, to treat my migraines."[11] As a young child, Wiesel often missed school because he was afraid to

Anti-Semitism had been in Europe for hundreds of years. This fifteenth-century woodcut shows Jews being burned during the Spanish Inquisition.

leave his mother. His earliest memory, about age three, is sitting on his bed calling for her.[12]

Sarah sang songs to comfort Elie, songs about the coming of the Messiah. Many Jews, including Sarah Wiesel, believe that the Messiah will come one day to save and lead the Jewish people to the Promised Land. "Fear not, my child. There will be no more armies," she sang as she rocked her son to sleep. Sarah Feig Wiesel graduated from high school in a time when few young women went past elementary school. She spoke several languages and memorized and quoted the modern German writers Goethe and Schiller.[13]

By all accounts, Elie's mother and father had a happy marriage. In fact, gossip said that Shlomo had fallen in love with her before they were married, something that was not supposed to happen. In that time and place, Jewish matchmakers usually determined marriages, not emotions. One evening, Shlomo saw a beautiful woman riding by in a carriage and ran after her, calling, "Who are you?" Of course, she did not reply, but that evening, the driver gave him the answer. She was Sarah, the younger daughter of Dodye Feig of the village of Bichkev. Shlomo and Sarah were married a year later.[14]

Every summer, the Wiesel family took a vacation in the nearby mountain village of Borsha. During the week, Elie stayed with his mother and sisters. Their father came at the end of each week. There, Elie remembers playing chess and taking long walks in the mountains.

Wiesel's love of music was born in those mountains. He took violin lessons twice a week from a police captain. Elie arrived with a bottle of *cuika* (plum wine), a gift to the teacher from his father. When the bottle was finished, so was the lesson. To please his father, Elie also sang in the synagogue's choir.

Dodye Feig (18??–1944?)

Wiesel's maternal grandfather, Dovid "Dodye" Feig, was a mountain in his grandson's eyes. With ruddy cheeks and a long white beard, he lived in a village near Sighet called Bichkev. He could tame wild horses on one hand and discuss Jewish philosophy on the other.

Elie loved his grandfather's farm. There, he felt free and easy. No one criticized him or judged him. He picked apricots and plums and helped his grandfather tend the cows and gardens.

Dodye Feig was a Hasidic Jew. This sect of Judaism was founded in the 1730s. Hasidism preaches joy against despair and spreads its teachings through legends and song. Hasids sing and pray loudly and dramatically, and believe in mysticism, or meditation, as a way of knowing God. Today, Wiesel believes that there is a revival of Hasidism in the world.[15]

To Elie, this grandfather was the perfect balance between the physical and the spiritual. He was also a peacemaker and a marvelous singer. Wiesel recalls him dressed in a long robe and a fur hat on Rosh Hashanah, the Jewish New Year, in 1943. He sang all the way from the synagogue back to their house, stopping only to call out "Happy New Year!" to everyone he saw. He brought Jewish stories to life with a loud voice and wide eyes. Wiesel has never forgotten those stories. He tells them over and over in his books.

Although young Elie worshipped his father, the children did not see much of him during the week. They *did* see him every week on Shabbat (the Sabbath). From Friday's sunset until the time on Saturday when three stars can be seen in the sky, Jewish families did no work. Together, they went to synagogue, prayed, ate, told stories, sang, and learned from holy books. Elie recalls:

> After the ritual bath we would walk to services, dressed for the occasion. Sometimes my father would take my hand, as though to protect me, as we passed the nearby police station or the central prison on the main square. I liked it when he did that, and I like to remember it now. I felt reassured, content. Bound to me, he belonged to me.[16]

In his memoirs, Elie admits that when he was a young child, he wanted his father all to himself and that he was jealous of the store and the community. In his seventies, Wiesel regretted that he never knew his father well while they lived at home in Sighet.[17]

Wiesel clearly recalls the night that his little sister Tzipora was born. His mother was in the throes of a long and difficult labor. Grandma Nissel sent six-year-old Elie to Rabbi Borcher's house to pray for help. A rabbi is the spiritual head of a Jewish congregation, a scholar and teacher who can offer advice and answers. The rabbi recited one psalm, then another, and then a third. Elie returned home to hear his grandmother ordering his mother to cry and shout, but the poor laboring woman was silent. Elie returned to the rabbi and explained that the prayers had not worked, that his mother would not shout. The rabbi prayed again. Soon Sarah's scream pierced the air. The rabbi smiled.[18]

Outside the Wiesel house stood an acacia tree under which Elie liked to sit and read. In the first volume of his memoirs,

All Rivers Run to the Sea, Wiesel recalls an afternoon when he sat watching the clouds while Tzipora played nearby with a hoop. She asked her brother to join her, but he was too preoccupied. Today, he regrets having said no.

In addition to recalling his family in his memoirs, Wiesel recalls his closest friends. There was Itzu Junger, who shared a tutor with Elie and lived in a luxurious house near the synagogue. There was Haimi Kahan, a strong, good-natured young man with whom Elie always felt safe. There was Chaim-Hersh who sang with a lovely baritone, and Itzu Goldblatt, with whom Elie competed in everything, except sports.

Sports held no interest for Elie; he never even learned to swim. He preferred chess and cards and long walks—and he loved to read. His first teacher, the white-haired Batizer Rebbe, introduced him to the Hebrew alphabet: "Here, children, are the beginning and the end of all things. Thousands upon thousands of works have been written and will be written with these letters. Look at them and study them with love, for they will be your links to life. And to eternity."[19]

In Elie's case, the rabbi's words were prophetic. As he learned to read, the ancient Jewish texts lit his imagination. When he read the legends and tales, it was as if he lived in two places and times at once. He lost himself in books. For young Elie Wiesel, reading offered the solitude he seemed to crave. It also offered his mind the freedom to soar.

The World Outside

European political lines were drawn and redrawn as power shifted. At the turn of the nineteenth century, Sighet was called Máramarossziget, and it belonged to the Austro-Hungarian Empire. When Elie was born in 1928, it was called Sighetul Marmatiei and belonged to the Kingdom of Greater Romania. Today, it is part of Hungary once again. During these transitions, except for the flags and the anthems, the town changed little. In the 1930s, Elie's sense of the world expanded from smaller to bigger, from inside to outside, and from Sighet to Europe.

When Elie was an adolescent, he suffered an attack of appendicitis. He needed surgery right away but it was the Sabbath, a day when Jews were forbidden to travel. His parents rushed to ask the rabbi's advice. Thankfully, the rabbi answered that they could travel if a life was at stake, so Wiesel's parents rushed him to the Jewish hospital in Satu Mare. Wiesel remembers having a crush on a kind young nurse who took care of him there.[20]

Elie believed that when he thought about girls, it was Satan leading him down the wrong path. Once, he saw a beautiful actress on a movie poster and her image occupied his thoughts, especially when he tried to sleep. When this happened, Elie disciplined himself with more and more study and prayer.

Although his sisters went to high school in Sighet, Elie's mother envisioned that he would one day be a *doktor rabiener,* a rabbi with a doctoral degree. Consequently, he was sent to a Jewish high school, first in Debrecen and later in Nagyvárad. His mother had great faith that her son would be a great man and a great teacher.

When Elie was eight years old, his mother brought him to be blessed by the famous Rabbi Israel of Wizhnitz. The rabbi took Elie into his arms and asked questions about his studies. When the young boy stammered and stuttered, the rabbi asked Sarah Wiesel to leave them alone. The rabbi spoke with young Eliezer for a long time. Later, when the rabbi spoke to Sarah in private, she burst into tears. Elie imagined that he must have said something horrible to the rabbi and felt very ashamed.

Twenty-five years later, Elie Wiesel met his cousin, Anshel Feig, who told him that he knew what had happened during the meeting between his mother and the rabbi. She had sworn Anshel to secrecy. The rabbi had said to her, "Sarah, know that your son will become a *gadol b'Israel*, a great man in Israel, but neither you nor I will live to see the day."[21]

Yellow Stars

In the evenings during the 1930s, the Wiesel family closed the shutters and listened to radio broadcasts. They heard classical and modern music, entertaining stories, and, of course, the news. They heard reports of the demise of the League of Nations, Stalin's rise to power in Russia, devastating floods in China, and a new military government in Japan. They also heard news from neighboring Germany and a name that they had never heard before: Adolf Hitler. He was the leader of a small but growing political organization called the National Socialist German Workers' party, commonly known as the Nazis.

Hitler's Rise to Power

In 1930, when Elie Wiesel was a toddler in Sighet, severe economic strife had hit Germany, part of a worldwide depression that began in 1929. Millions of unemployed Germans stood in breadlines as the German *deutschmark*

The symbol of Hitler's Nazi Party was the Swastika.

plummeted in value. Amidst the chaos of a collapsing economy, a young, dark-haired speaker named Adolf Hitler offered hope and promise to crowds who gathered to hear his passionate words. His repeated denunciations of Jewish businesses and wealth touched a nerve among poor Germans who were eager to find a scapegoat for their misfortunes. A group of his followers, called the Brownshirts, attacked Jewish civilians in Berlin in January, killing eight.[1] Among the most feared members of the Nazi party were the black-uniformed protection squad, known as the *Schutzstaffel*, or SS. As members of the SS stood guard, Hitler worked a crowd into deliriums of hatred with his "pounding fists, burning eyes, hoarse cries and hysterics."[2] An eyewitness named Ericka Mann wrote, "I have never heard any other speaker who was so able to penetrate into the soul of the individual . . . You cannot imagine how silent it becomes as soon as this man speaks; it is as if all of the thousand listeners are no longer able to breathe."[3]

In 1930, many political parties vied for power in the Reichstag, the German lawmaking body. Nazis held only 12 seats in 1930, but this number increased to 107 in 1931. In March 1931, Hitler sent this directive to all Nazi officials: "The natural hostility of the peasant against the Jews . . . must be worked up to a frenzy."[4] As history shows, the officials obeyed the order. By 1932, the Nazis held 230 seats in the Reichstag. In September of that year, Alfred Rosenberg, editor of the Nazi party newspaper, announced the party's plan for the country: All Germans were to be consolidated into one German state in which no Jew could remain a citizen.

By many historians' accounts, 1933 was a turning point of the twentieth century. By then, the Nazis had gained more legislative seats than any other party. On January 30, 1933,

Adolf Hitler
(1889–1945)

Adolf Hitler was born in Austria, the fourth of six children. His abusive father died when Adolf was fourteen; his mother, four years later. When he was young, Adolf wanted to be a painter. He quit school and later moved to Vienna, working odd jobs, applying to art schools, and selling small paintings.

Many Jews lived in Vienna and to Hitler, they were not German. To him, they were barely human. By the time Adolf Hitler moved to Munich, Germany, in 1913, his hatred of Jews had become an obsession.

In 1914, World War I began, and Hitler enlisted in the German army. The German army was defeated, however, and Hitler was one of the many who returned to Germany a bitter, hateful man. Hitler—and many others—blamed the Communists and the Jews.

Hitler joined the National Socialist German Workers', or Nazi, party and soon realized a new talent: public speaking. He sometimes rented a dozen beer halls and ran from one to the next delivering impassioned speeches. Soon, he was addressing crowds of thousands. He also wrote a book, *Mein Kampf (My Struggle)*. In it, he details his goals: especially expelling the Jews from Germany. In his book, he calls the Jew a "parasite."[5]

By 1933, he was dictator of Germany and the Nazis were the only official party allowed in the country.

Adolf Hitler became the chancellor of Germany. Within a year, he evolved into a ruthless dictator who ruled with brutality and unwavering certainty. German children were required to join groups called Hitler Youth, which stressed unwavering obedience and military discipline. Jews were removed from all civil service and teaching posts. In April, Nazis began to boycott all Jewish businesses. Quickly, Hitler's hatred of Jews became public policy. His desire that Germany be free of Jews turned into law. His dream of a world without Jews became his plan.

The German word for empire is *Reich*. Hitler believed that the first great German Reich was from 962 to 1806. The second was from 1871 through World War I. Hitler's reign was known as the Third Reich. He imagined that it would last for a thousand years. He began by creating anti-Jewish laws. Jews could not work in the arts or practice law in German courts. Jewish doctors could not practice in German hospitals. In May 1933, Berlin University students burned seventy thousand tons of books by "undesirable writers." In 1935, new laws forbade marriages and sexual relations between Jews and Germans and forbade Jews to display the German flag.

Also in 1935, Hitler began to build his armies and sent troops to Germany's farthest borders in blatant violation of the Treaty of Versailles, the international agreement in 1919 that officially ended World War I. The other European leaders objected to Germany's violations, but their fear of starting another world war kept them from intervening. In March

---

Book burnings were common in Nazi Germany during the 1930s.

1938, Nazi troops marched triumphantly into Austria after conspirators assassinated the country's leader. In 1939, Hitler's army occupied Czechoslovakia. By this time, the leaders of Great Britain and France realized that Hitler meant to conquer Europe and that he must be stopped. Hitler's armies invaded Poland on September 1, 1939. When Britain and France declared war on Germany on September 3, World War II ignited.

By this time, Germany controlled regions that were home to millions of Jews. At first, Hitler planned to expel them all, that is, to deport them from Europe to Madagascar, off southeastern Africa.[6] As Germany gained control over more of Europe, however, this became impractical. Where would they all go?

The Jews of Sighet were frightened by what they heard. Hitler was a fire on the horizon; his flame grew closer as months went by. Everyone knew that Hitler and his Nazi party hated Jews, but in 1939, no one imagined how far their hatred could go. To Elie Wiesel in Sighet, Hitler and his armies were not yet real. They were just stories on the radio, whispered conversations among his father's friends, the fears of adults that bore no relevance to the lives of the young.

Elie's Obsession

Like most boys his age, Elie cared about girls, but in his imagination only. He also began to develop his lifelong love of music, but what he loved most was reading and studying. With his closest friends, he shared a fascination with the study of Jewish texts. This interest took two paths: the traditional and the occult.

Like most Jewish youth before him—and many since—Elie prepared intensely for the most important day of his young Jewish life. In their thirteenth year, Jewish boys participate in a ritual called a bar mitzvah, through which they become adults in the eyes of their community and are obligated to keep 613 *mitzvoth*, or commandments. In a public ceremony, the boy stands before all the members of the synagogue and reads the Shabbat passage from the Torah. Then he gives a speech in which he interprets the passage he has just read. In 1941, Elie Wiesel's bar mitzvah was celebrated by the Rebbe of Borsha in a synagogue right across the street from his home. In this service, Wiesel became "a responsible adult, a full-fledged member of the community of Israel."[7] His whole family—including Elie himself—was very proud.

Elie was also interested in a more mysterious study: collected mystical writings known as the Cabala. Usually, people do not read and discuss the Cabala until they are adults, but Elie and two of his friends wanted to seek this "hidden wisdom" when they were very young men. His father did not approve of this path, but Elie pursued it anyway.

The Cabala is a belief system expressed and explored in ancient written texts. Like philosophy, it is the study of large philosophical ideas: the meaning of life and the relationship of matter and spirit. The Cabala speaks of miracles, divinity, creation, the role of humans, and the fate of the soul. Cabalists search for patterns and geometric puzzles in the ancient texts with the belief that secrets are buried in the details. Like holy actors, they retell myths and legends.

These were not the usual subjects of study for young people. Yet Elie and his friends learned, talked, thought, and dreamed about them with the kind of obsessive devotion natural to adolescents.

> Astrology, magic, morphology, hypnotism, graphology, parapsychology, alchemy. In short, I became entranced by what lay beyond reality. With a little luck, I thought, I would learn how to turn dust into gold, danger into

security, harmless gestures into acts of war against war. I was fascinated by the mystical experiences, or alleged mystical experiences, recounted in these books yellowed by the centuries.[8]

One day, a barefoot man approached Elie in the synagogue and the two began to talk. Elie said that he was seeking a teacher who knew the Cabala. This strange-looking man named Moché became that teacher. Together, they spent long hours discussing principles, revelations, and mysteries. Moché was a unique character; he sang and laughed; there was light in his eyes. It was Moché who taught Elie that wisdom resides in questions, not answers.

As Elie and his friends sought wisdom from within, the news from without both worsened and horrified. The threat of Hitler and his anti-Semitic rule was moving closer to home. To the north and west, the Nazis invaded and now occupied France and parts of the Netherlands and Belgium. Elie and two of his friends, Yiddele and Sruli, kept a huge map of Europe on which Yiddele marked the latest battles and advances. "The German advance is like lightning," Yiddele observed, "a fearsome unstoppable tactic."[9] In fact, the Germans called their warfare *blitzkrieg*, which means "lightning war." As the war became more real to them, the three friends looked to the Cabala to find answers.

Shlomo Wiesel disapproved of his son's obsession, but he agreed to let it continue as long as his study of the Torah did not suffer. Elie and his friends met in secret until one day, Yiddele fell gravely ill. He lost the ability to speak and the will to live. Eventually, he recovered, but doctors and grown-ups

Members of a Jewish community in Sighet, Romania, pose for a group portrait, sometime in the 1930s.

blamed the illness on the boys' obsessive behavior. Then, Sruli took sick with the same symptoms. Elie's father suggested that it was a curse. Young Elie promised to be more careful. He believed that if he prayed fervently enough, and studied hard enough, a Messiah would save the Jews—and the world—from Hitler.

In His Own Backyard

All the prayers and all the study seemed to do no good. Soon, blatant acts of anti-Semitism began to happen in Sighet. Groups of thugs assaulted Jews while the local police looked on.[10] For their safety, Jews hurried their children off the streets at nightfall.

In 1940, Shlomo Wiesel was arrested. He had helped Jews who fled from Poland after Hitler's invasion. One refugee was later captured and, during his interrogation, mentioned Shlomo Wiesel's name. As a result, Shlomo spent two months in prison, first in Sighet, then in Debrecen. In June 1941, German armies invaded Russia and the war escalated to new heights. In December 1941, the Japanese dropped bombs on Pearl Harbor and the United States entered the war.

The war crept closer and closer to the rural villages of southern Europe—and then, it reached Sighet. In 1942, the government expelled all the foreign Jews, including Elie's beloved teacher, Moché. Police crammed thousands of these foreign Jews into trains. At first, people back in Sighet believed that the deportees had been taken to nearby labor camps and were being treated and fed well.

Weeks passed. One day, as Elie walked to the synagogue, he saw Moché. The man had changed. His eyes were dark and he did not laugh or sing. He only spoke of what he had seen.

Moché told Elie that the trains had taken them into Poland. There, the German police loaded them onto trucks, drove them into a forest, and forced them to dig enormous pits. Then, the police lined up Moché and the others and shot them so that they fell into what became mass graves. Babies were thrown into the air and shot down by machine gunners. Moché managed to escape by playing dead, then hiding in the woods and making his way home.

No one believed Moché's story, including Elie. Everyone thought he was insane. Moché told the tale to anyone who would listen, weeping as he spoke. He tried to warn the Jews of Sighet, but no one would pay attention.

The Jews of Sighet had no idea what was planned for them. No one had heard of the Wannsee Conference. On January 20, 1942, fourteen senior Nazi officials met in a secluded lakeside villa in Berlin. SS General Adolf Eichmann handed each participant a list of all European countries and the numbers of Jews who lived in each, totaling more than 11 million.[11] Conference leader SS General Reinhard Heydrich explained that the goal of the current government was that all countries under Nazi rule would be completely *Judenfrei* (free of Jews). They called their plan the "Final Solution of the Jewish Question." The Nazis would methodically kill them all—every single Jewish father, mother, daughter, and son.

The next year, 1943, passed quietly for Elie Wiesel. By day, he studied the Talmud, the collected Jewish laws, commentaries, and teachings. By night, his mind was still on the Cabala. His father continued to help refugees. His mother wondered about a husband for her daughter, Bea. The Jewish New Year came and went. The Allied nations had invaded Italy, and the Russians were beginning to defeat the German army in the east. It seemed as if the war in Europe would end soon. Although they could hear bombs in the distance, the family—and the village—seemed safe.

The Ghetto

In March 1944, the radio announced that a new government had taken over Budapest, the capital of Hungary. Perhaps it was just a change in administration, Elie's family hoped. The following day, however, German troops marched into Hungary. Three days later, German army cars rumbled through the streets of Sighet.

German soldiers took up temporary residence in private homes; some even stayed with Jewish families. They were polite; some, even charming. The Jews of Sighet were relieved. With spring came Passover, the Jewish holiday that commemorates the Jews' exodus from slavery in ancient Egypt. That year, the synagogues were closed. After the holiday, the Jews learned that they could not leave their homes for three days—or they would be killed.

During this time, Hungarian police burst into Jewish homes and confiscated gold, jewels, and other valuables. Elie's father hid the family savings in the basement. The family buried their most precious possessions in the backyard, under a tree.

Three days later, a new law decreed that every Jew must sew a yellow star onto his or her clothing. Jews could not eat in restaurants, ride trains, or be out on the street after 6:00 P.M. Whoever disobeyed these new orders would be shot. People could hardly believe what they read on the posters: "Shot." Right there in black and white it said they could be killed.

Soon, the occupying Germans created two ghettos in Sighet, forced all the Jews inside their perimeters, and surrounded them with barbed wire. The larger ghetto was in the center of town and included the Wiesel home, so the family did not have to move, but relatives moved in with them. The men of the ghetto set up a Jewish government and Jewish police. The self-containment almost seemed like a blessing. They assumed they would live like this until the war ended—and of course, that would be any day.[12]

In April 1944, the Wiesels' beloved housekeeper, Maria, a gentile (non-Jew), begged them to flee to her home in the mountains. They could hide there until the war ended. There would be room for the whole family, she assured them, even Grandma Nissel. She would bring them food, and they would be safe. But the family said no. Maria's life would be in danger if she were caught hiding Jews. More importantly, the Wiesels did not want to leave their community. In the ghetto, everyone took care of everyone else.

One day, however, everything changed. Elie's father was summoned to a meeting of the Judenrat, the Jewish Council. Rumors began to circulate; there was talk about "transports" to the east. Shlomo returned with one chilling word: "Deportation." The Jews of Sighet must leave their village, beginning the following day. They could take only a few personal items with them. And no one knew where they were going.

4

Death Trains

The Nazis organized the deportations by groups. The next morning, the first groups prepared to leave. Mothers baked bread. Fathers packed small belongings. Children said good-bye. Once they were in the street, the Jews were not allowed to return to their homes, even if they were thirsty. The Wiesels were not among the first groups to leave Sighet. As their neighbors waited in the hot streets, Elie and his little sister, Tzipora, went among them with pots and ladles, giving out drinks of water.

Elie watched the first groups of Jews march out of Sighet. On everyone's back was a pack. Teachers, rabbis, friends, whole families, young and old—they all marched in a slow procession through the ghetto gates to the trains.

After the first deportees left Sighet, those who remained in the ghetto could hear and see the Soviet armies in the mountains only a few miles away. As they fought to stop Hitler's army, their artillery lit the sky like fireworks. During that night, someone knocked on the door of the Wiesel home. It was Maria, who again begged them to flee to safety. Still, Elie's father said no. "A Jew must never be separated from his community," he explained to the kind woman. "What happens to everyone else will happen to us as well."[1] There was some talk of sending the children with Maria, but the family decided to stay together.

Their turn came on Tuesday, May 16, 1944. Again, everyone was thirsty as they waited in the hot sun for hours. Tzipora's lips were dry and parched. At last the order came: "Forward! March!" Everyone began to move. "Faster you lazy swine!" the Hungarian police yelled. If they did not move quickly enough, the police hit them with sticks. They began to run, not knowing to where. As they ran, Elie saw his father cry for the first time.

Finally, they reached the smaller ghetto. The German soldiers told them that they would be there for only a few days. Exhausted, yet happy to still be in Sighet, they moved into the home of Uncle Mendel, Shlomo's brother. Sarah Wiesel cooked potato pancakes. That night, they ate as much as they wanted. While they were in the "little ghetto," Maria appeared a third time. Again, the Wiesels refused to be separated from their community or from each other.

On Saturday—the Sabbath—the Nazis marched the Jews of Sighet to the synagogue. They locked them in, men downstairs, women upstairs, with hardly enough air to breathe and no bathrooms to use.

Twenty-four hours later, the Nazis marched them to the train station where the cattle cars waited. The soldiers packed about eighty Jews into each car with a few loaves of bread and some buckets of water. In each car, one person was in charge. Anyone trying to escape would be shot. The doors were sealed. The whistle screamed. The heavy train wheels moved . . . first slowly . . . then picking up speed, then faster—and then with tremendous force.

"Life in the cattle cars was the death of my adolescence."[2]

Under Nazi control, Elie Wiesel's world grew smaller and smaller and smaller. "The country became a city, the city a street, the street a house, the house a room, the room a sealed cattle car."[3]

Despite the fact that the Nazis paid full passenger fares for each Jew who rode these trains, the passengers were not treated as passengers but as freight. These train cars could hold eight horses or forty soldiers, but the Nazis packed as many as one hundred Jews in each car for journeys that typically lasted several days. No one could sit or lie down. The only light came from one small opening covered with bars or wire. People relieved themselves in the corners. In the winter, many victims froze to death. In the summer, they died from thirst, heat, or even suffocation. It was not uncommon for a train carrying a thousand Jews to arrive at its destination with two hundred people already dead.

The German railroad companies made a fortune. The Nazis paid a reduced rate for groups of four hundred or more, but they transported millions. The money came from the sale of all the property they confiscated from the Jews. Children under ten were half price; under four traveled free. Of course, these were all one way tickets, except for the guards.

Jews often died from heat exhaustion, suffocation, dehydration, and suicide in trains while on their way to concentration camps.

Many diaries by German citizens during the 1940s include eerie descriptions of the endless death trains that rattled and puffed through central Europe all day and night. Even when Germany began to lose the war, the trains still operated with chilling efficiency—right on time, according to their tight schedules.[4]

On the second day, the Wiesels' train stopped at the town of Kaschau, on the Czechoslovak border, and the door was opened. A German soldier announced that they were now under the authority of the German army. He wore the uniform of a SS officer, now the most elite soldiers in the Third Reich. The officer ordered the Jews to surrender whatever possessions they carried. As a Hungarian lieutenant walked among them with a basket, people dropped in watches and coins. "If anyone is missing, you'll all be shot, like dogs!" the lieutenant yelled just before the door was slammed and nailed shut.[5]

The heat was intense; the air, scant; and the closed cars smelled of sweat and human waste. The ride drove some people insane. One of these was Madame Schachter who had been separated from her husband and all sons but one. She screamed "Fire! I can see a fire!" when there was nothing in front of her but darkness. Madame Schachter's wild screams took their toll on others in the car. Several young men tied and gagged her to silence her, for everyone in the train was at his or her breaking point. She escaped from restraint only to scream more. "Flames! Flames!" People hit her to make her quiet. Finally, she crouched in a corner in a bewildered gaze.[6]

After five days, the train stopped. The men near the window read the name of the station: Auschwitz. The train sat still for the afternoon, and finally guards opened the doors. Two men were allowed to fetch water. When they returned, they said that a guard told them that this was their last stop. Auschwitz was a concentration camp and the conditions here were good. Families would not be split up, they said, and only the young people would have to work. For the first time in many days, the Jews of Sighet felt hope.[7] Night fell. The wheels began to move again.

When the train stopped, Madame Schachter screamed again, but this time, when the men looked out the window, they saw flames gushing from a chimney. The doors opened. Men holding torches ordered them out. It was midnight.

They had arrived at Auschwitz-Birkenau. Auschwitz began as a concentration camp in 1940, but by 1942, it had become a death camp. There were six death camps in Nazi-occupied Europe, all located in Poland: Chelmno, Auschwitz, Belzec, Sobibor, Treblinka, and Maidanek. In these camps, labor was not the object; murder was. Their sole purpose was to kill people the Nazis considered undesirable—mostly Jews. More than a third of the Jews murdered in the Holocaust died in the six death camps. Auschwitz-Birkenau was the largest of all. In fact, it was the largest single center of mass murder in human history.

As they jumped from the train, the Jews of Sighet sensed a horrible smell that most could not name. The smell came from the enormous chimney. The Nazis burned the bodies of their victims in huge furnaces called crematories. The smell was burning human flesh. Like the trains, the crematories ran with frightening efficiency. A person could arrive at Auschwitz at sunrise, and by sunset, his or her corpse would be cremated, his or her clothing shipped to Germany.[8]

"Men to the left! Women to the right!"[9]

The Wiesel family walked away from the train holding each other's hands. Veteran prisoners yelled at them for being there: "You'd have done better to have hanged yourself where you were than come here. Didn't you know what was in store for you at Auschwitz?"[10] Every few yards, an SS soldier pointed a machine gun at them. An officer barked the order for men and women to separate: "Men to the left! Women to the right!" Elie held his father's hand as they did what they were told. "For a part of a second I glimpsed my mother and my sisters moving away to the right. Tzipora held Mother's hand. I saw them disappear into the distance; my mother was stroking my sister's fair hair, as though to protect her, while I walked on with my father and the other men."[11]

Soon, another SS officer ordered the men to form groups of five. One of the prisoners asked Wiesel how old he was. When Elie answered "Fifteen," the man said he should lie and tell them that he was eighteen. When Wiesel's father said he was fifty, the man said to lie and say he was forty. "Eighteen and forty," he instructed them and then vanished.[12]

Nazi guards forced the prisoners into the square in the middle of the camp. There, Dr. Josef Mengele, the chief medical officer of the camp, stood holding a music conductor's baton. The prisoners called him "The Angel of Death." As the prisoners filed past him, Mengele pointed the baton to either the left or the right to indicate whether they would live or die. When Elie stepped forward, the doctor asked him his age. "Eighteen," he said. The baton moved to the left. Elie Wiesel had just passed his first selection.

Next, it was Shlomo's turn. The baton moved to the left again. They were together. It was a blessing. As they walked ahead, they saw huge flames rising from a ditch. The soldiers lead them toward what looked to Elie like the pit of hell. Trucks were driving to the edge, delivering something that was being dumped into the pit. At one point, Elie was only a

Adolf Eichmann
(1906–1962)

Adolf Eichmann was born near Cologne, Germany. His family moved to Austria following his mother's death. Despite the fact that he was not Jewish, kids teased him for his dark skin and called him "little Jew."

In 1932, Eichmann joined the SS. He was assigned to collect information on Jews. He soon became the "Jewish specialist," assigned to explore "solutions to the Jewish question." At first, in 1937, he explored sending Jews out of Europe.

In 1939, Adolf Eichmann was appointed head of Gestapo Section IV B4 for Jewish Affairs. With fanatical efficiency, he ran the train systems that delivered millions of people to the camps in order to accomplish the "Final Solution." By August 1944, Eichmann reported that 4 million Jews had died in the death camps and 2 million others had been killed by mobile units.

When the war ended, Eichmann was arrested but escaped. He fled to Argentina and lived in hiding. In 1960, Israeli agents captured him after he was located by survivor and Nazi-hunter Simon Wiesenthal. Over one hundred witnesses, including many Holocaust survivors, testified against him in a trial in Jerusalem. Eichmann was found guilty of crimes against Jews and humanity, sentenced to death, and hanged on May 31, 1962.

few steps away and could see what they were doing: The Nazis were throwing Jewish babies into the burning pit—alive.

Ten years later, in his book *Night,* Wiesel describes that first night in the camp. This haunting passage is perhaps the most famous written by a Holocaust survivor.

> Never shall I forget that night . . . which has turned my life into one long night . . . Never shall I forget that smoke. Never shall I forget the little faces of the children, whose bodies I saw turned into wreaths of smoke beneath a silent blue sky . . . Never.[13]

On that first night in Auschwitz-Birkenau—and for the first time in his young life—Elie Wiesel began to question God. In many ways, he has never stopped.

Work or Die

The men were forced to strip naked. They had to throw their clothes into a huge heap and stand in the cold with only their shoes and their belts in their hands. Next, their heads and bodies were shaved. For hours, they comforted each other, thankful to be together.

That night, the Nazis forced them to run in a cold wind to another wooden barracks. There, they were disinfected and sprayed with hot water, and sent outside again. The Nazis forced them into another barracks where guards issued prison clothes. As morning broke, the Jews of Sighet could barely recognize each other. Finally, an SS officer came in and spoke.

....

Those who were not killed when they came to concentration camps were often put to work. However, those who worked were usually starved and worked to the point of death.

The officer explained to the new inmates that they were in Auschwitz-Birkenau. Here they had two choices: to work or to die in the crematories. Electricians, locksmiths, and watchmakers were separated from everyone else. The rest were sent to another barracks and, finally, got to sit down.

Shlomo was suddenly sick to his stomach. When he asked for the bathroom, a guard struck him with such force that he came crawling back to his son. Elie watched it all, but he took no action to defend his father. Already, after only a few hours in the camp, he was changing.

The next day was a beautiful spring day. The guards forced them to run to the main part of the camp—Auschwitz I. Together, Elie and Shlomo ran through an iron door with these words inscribed above: ARBEIT MACHT FREI! (WORK MAKES FREE!)

Their first impression made them feel hopeful. They saw three-story brick barracks instead of wooden ones. They saw little gardens here and there. They were led to another barracks to wait again. Again, they showered and had to stand shivering in the cold night air. Toward midnight, they were ordered to run to yet another barracks.

At the barracks, a young Polish supervisor greeted them and spoke kindly. He encouraged them to have faith, not to despair, and to help one another. To the exhausted Wiesels, these words were the first bit of human decency in what seemed like hell itself. Father and son climbed into a wooden bunk and slept.

5

The Longest Night

At 6:00 A.M., a bell woke everyone up. They drank coffee. They washed and got new uniforms. For lunch: a thin, saltless soup. Elie refused to eat his, so his father ate his portion. In the afternoon they were allowed to rest. Then, one by one, they filed past men who tattooed blue numbers on their left arms with needles. Elie became A–7713.

Elie and his father lived in a barracks called a block with about two thousand other men. These buildings were huge, rectangular, sturdy, and functional. Each block contained about five hundred bunks, four men per bunk. These bare wooden planks looked more like shelves than beds. Each was covered with dirty straw. Lice and fleas crawled everywhere, bearing and spreading the deadly diseases typhus and dysentery that claimed the lives of thousands. The buildings were stifling hot in the summer; freezing in the winter. Buckets served as toilets.

By the third day, Wiesel ate everything. Hunger pains nagged him constantly. The Nazis barely provided enough food to keep them alive. Thin black coffee in the morning. Watery soup at the noon bell. At the 6:00 P.M. bell: roll call, then dinner, which was bread with margarine or jam. At 9:00 P.M. , a bell signaled bed. For three weeks, this is how it went. Sometimes men sang Hasidic songs. Every Shabbat they prayed together. They told stories. They often spoke of the coming of the Messiah. Elie and Shlomo wondered about Sarah, Bea, Hilda, and Tzipora, hoping they were safe, but silently fearing the worst.[1]

All the skilled workers went to other camps and, finally, it was their turn to move on. One day, after coffee and roll call, the Nazis forced them to march out of the camp and onto the road. About one hundred inmates from the concentration camp walked through villages. After a four-hour march, the prisoners reached a new camp, Buna-Monowitz (Auschwitz III), a sub-camp of the Auschwitz complex.

They learned that the Nazis were putting them in quarantine but planning to put them to work. More days passed. Their hunger remained constant and intense. Prisoners held onto their last crusts of bread, unsure there would be more. Elie—and everyone else—lost more and more weight. Soon, they were mostly skin and bone.

At first, the work was not hard. They sorted and counted bolts, bulbs, and electrical fittings. Wiesel worked beside his father, and in addition, he made friends in Buna with two Czech brothers about his age. With Elie, they talked of Eretz Y'israel (the Land of Israel) and sang songs. They predicted that the war would end within weeks. They only had to hold out a little while longer.

Sometimes, Elie played chess with other prisoners—without a board or pieces. They played by memory. To this day, he plays chess alone.

Days turned into weeks. Wiesel lost track of time. All he thought about was soup and bread. Elie and his father were always together. They became one another's best friend and each other's reason for staying alive.

Once, Elie stumbled upon a Nazi foreman having sex with a young girl. Soon, the Nazi called out, "A-7713!" Elie had to lie on his stomach on a box in front of all the others. The soldier whipped him—twenty-five lashes—until he fainted.

Another time, a Nazi beat Shlomo, and Elie did nothing to stop it. If he had, the Nazis would have beat him, too. But there was another reason: Fear and starvation were killing his compassion. He even felt angry with his father for not avoiding the beating.[2]

Supervisors were chosen from among the prisoners and called kapos. Some tried to be humane when the Nazis were not watching, but others were brutal. One day, the kapo demanded the gold crown on Elie's tooth. Elie held him off for several days, but finally, he felt so threatened—for both himself and his father—that he gave in. A dentist pulled his tooth with a rusty spoon.

Bombs, Gallows, and a New Year

One Sunday, Elie and his father were resting in the barracks when the air-raid siren went off. All of the guards ran for the shelters. They left two huge cauldrons of soup out in the open, unguarded.

One prisoner crawled to the soup. Overhead, American planes bombed Buna. As he bent over the hot cauldron, one of the planes' bombs killed him. However, Elie was not afraid of the bombs. He had lost his fear of death. He rejoiced at the sound of the bombs. They offered the promise of destroying the Nazis. But after an hour, the planes were gone. The man at the cauldron was the only casualty. The next day the prisoners had to move a live bomb out of the camp. They also had to clear the wreckage—but cleaning up even a small degree of destruction of Nazi property was a task they completed "cheerfully."[3]

In the camps, the Nazis sometimes executed prisoners by hanging, mostly as a warning to the others. Attendance by all prisoners was mandatory. In *Night*, Wiesel recalls how the Nazis forced ten thousand prisoners to watch a strong young man hanged for stealing. Although he had witnessed the cremation of thousands, Elie was overwhelmed by this horrid spectacle. "Then the whole camp, block after block, had to march past the hanged man and stare at the dimmed eyes, the lolling tongue of death. The Kapos and heads of each block forced everyone to look him full in the face."[4]

One day, the prisoners returned from work to find three gallows built in the open assembly area. Three Dutch saboteurs had succeeded in blowing up an electric power station. Two were adults; one was a small child. The Nazis hanged all three at once. The two men died instantly, but the lightweight child did not. Thousands of prisoners filed by, looking at the child suspended between life and death for a long, long time. The experience made Elie question his faith, as he heard other prisoners around him ask, "Where is God now?"

Summer turned to fall in the camps. The Nazis transferred Elie to another unit. Now he was separated from his father. Every day, for twelve hours, he hauled huge heavy stone building blocks.

In September, Jewish prisoners observed the Jewish New Year. On the last night of this holiday, the prisoners in Elie's block saved their soup for after evening prayers. Ten thousand men gathered to say the prayers that Jews had been saying for thousands of years. Even in this hellish place, they praised God and sang of his greatness. Elie, however, could no longer pray. He felt empty. "My eyes were open and I was alone—terribly alone in a world without God and without man. Without love or mercy."[5]

During this period, the holiest time of the year for Jews, the SS scheduled another selection for the death chambers. Elie worried about his father, who seemed to have aged many years in the last few months. Elie had made two new friends, Tibi and Yossi, and the three of them stayed together during the selection. They had to remove all their clothes and run past Dr. Mengele, who held printed lists of numbers. He sent weak prisoners to the gas chambers to be killed. Elie ran as fast as he could past the "Angel of Death," too fast for anyone to see the number on his arm. When the selection was done, he ran to Block 36 to find his father. Miraculously, the Nazis had not chosen to kill Shlomo. To celebrate, Shlomo gave Elie a half-ration of bread for which he had traded a piece of rubber.

As winter came, conditions in the camp got worse and worse. The Nazis continued selections for the gas chambers. Rations were more meager. Many prisoners lost all faith and hope. There were more beatings. Elie's spirit and body were crushed and battered with backbreaking daily labor. He worked outdoors in thin clothing. Days grew colder and colder; nights grew longer and longer.

"Run!"

An icy wind blew through Buna. The prisoners were given slightly thicker striped shirts, but the stones that Elie moved were so cold that they made his hands ache.

In the middle of January 1945, Elie's right foot began to swell from an infection. He went to the camp hospital that was run by a Jewish doctor. He spent some days in a bed with

Josef Mengele
(1911–1978?)

Josef Mengele was serious and intelligent, even as a boy. He went to university and from there to medical school. He developed a particular interest in genetics, the science of how characteristics are passed from parents to children. His special interest was hereditary abnormalities. In 1937, he joined the SS. At Auschwitz, he became the chief medical officer, in charge of "selecting" which prisoners should live and which ones should die.

He often strutted around the camp with a riding crop in his right hand. Every day, he ordered new prisoners to parade naked in front of him. At Auschwitz, Mengele carried out inhumane studies on twins and dwarves. For prisoners, being a twin was a torturous means of survival. Nearly three thousand twins were part of Mengele's often grisly experiments. For example, in one, he dripped toxic chemicals into people's eyes in an attempt to change their color. Mengele hoped to use his research to try to create a master Aryan race.

After the war was over, Josef Mengele escaped to Argentina, where he was granted political asylum. In 1960, the German government asked that he be returned for trial. Mengele escaped to Brazil and later moved on to Paraguay. Many people believe that he drowned in Brazil in 1978. While bones found in 1985 were identified as his, some people believe he may still be alive.[6]

white sheets, something he had forgotten existed in the world. The soup was thicker in the hospital and the bread was better. He even had an operation. A kind doctor drained the pus from his foot, and he spent two weeks in the infirmary healing.

During those two weeks spent in recovery, the Russian army advanced closer and closer to the camp. The prisoners heard rumors that the Nazis would flee if the army got too close. One day, the Nazis announced that all prisoners—except those in the infirmary—would be moved. Elie was still recovering, but he went to find his father. They agreed that he would join the other prisoners and evacuate the camp. That night, Elie slept in his block although his bandaged foot was still bleeding. The snow turned red where he walked. His foot burned as if it were on fire.

The next day, all the prisoners were ordered to leave the camp. Everyone put on as much clothing as their emaciated bodies could possibly carry. To Elie, they all looked like pathetic clowns. He wrapped his swollen foot with a piece of cloth he tore from a blanket. Night fell, and on this night, it snowed. Searchlights blazed. Hundreds of SS guards surrounded the prisoners. The gates of the camp were opened, and the SS guards forced fifty-six blocks of men to march. In Elie's pocket were two pieces of bread.

As these tens of thousands of men marched, many fell, and many were trampled to death. The Nazis shot anyone who stepped out of line. Elie and Shlomo ran side by side. Their limbs went numb, but they kept running. As the morning star rose, the commandant announced that they had already covered forty-two miles. Finally, the Nazis allowed them to rest. Hundreds of men found shelter in an empty brick factory. For a while, Elie and his father slept.

When Elie woke, his father was staring at him. Shlomo was a broken and exhausted man who looked like a living corpse. Father and son stumbled outside and walked among the dead and dying. They returned to their shelter and dozed, woke, and dozed again as they tried to keep each other from sleeping, fearing that sleep meant freezing to death.

The Nazis ordered them to march again, and it snowed more. Numb with cold, Wiesel's foot no longer hurt. The guards had stopped shooting. They did not have to: With every step, a man fell.

Prisoners of concentration camps were starved and worked to the point of exhaustion.

Hours passed, and still, they kept marching. Suddenly, the gates of another sub-camp of Auschwitz-Gleiwitz loomed before them. As they pushed into the barracks, many men were trampled and crushed. At one point, Elie was crushed under so many bodies that he could not breathe. By some miracle, he clawed his way to air. Soon, he recognized his friend Juliek who had played the violin at Buna. Juliek, by another miracle, had carried his violin all this way.

Finally, in the barracks, the exhausted men lay in piles, as close to death as human beings can come. Juliek began to play a Beethoven concerto. The next morning, Juliek was dead, but Elie Wiesel and his father were still alive.

Two days after the evacuation of Buna, Wiesel learned later, the Russian army liberated the prisoners who had stayed behind in the hospital.

"Eliezer"

Elie and his father stayed at Gleiwitz for three days, but the prisoners were not allowed to leave the barracks. On the third day, at dawn, despite more snow, the guards forced the prisoners outdoors and made them leave the camp. With blankets around their shoulders, they marched. After half an hour, they stopped. The Nazis gave each man a piece of bread. It seemed like a feast. To quench his thirst, each man pulled out his spoon and ate the snow from his neighbor's back. The SS laughed at the sight. Hours later, a train arrived. The Nazis packed them in, one hundred to a car. This time the cattle cars had no roofs. And still, it snowed.

The next day, the train stopped in a field. The guards ordered the prisoners to throw out the dead. They nearly threw Shlomo into the snow until Elie yelled for him to wake up, and his father did. Once, Elie woke with someone's hands around his neck, trying to strangle him.

For ten days and ten nights they rode on this train. They had no bread, no food. They ate snow. The train passed slowly through German towns where the people stopped and stared. On occasion, some Germans threw bread into the train. The starving men stampeded and fought each other for crumbs. Once, Elie saw a father and son fight over one piece of bread: They both died in the battle. On the last day of the journey, a snowy wind blew. The prisoners wrapped their blankets more tightly and spun around to keep from freezing. Many died. At one point, everyone who had a voice cried out, wailing and groaning in absolute despair. Their screams mixed with the howling wind.

When they reached the new camp, Buchenwald, only a dozen of the hundred men who boarded ten days before walked off the car. Elie and Shlomo were among them. They took hot showers and went to their new barracks. In the distance, the chimneys of the crematories roared, but Elie hardly noticed. All he could think of was sleep. Sleep and food.

By this time, Shlomo was extremely weak and had nearly lost his spirit. Elie slept soundly that night. In the morning, his first thought was that his father was dead. Ashamed, he admitted to himself that this was not a fear—but a wish. If his father died, he would be more likely—and more able—to survive.

But no, Shlomo was still alive. Burning with fever, he begged his son for coffee. Elie worked all day, but in the

This photograph was taken three days after the liberation of Buchenwald. The prisoners volunteered to return to the barracks so that an American photographer could capture the overcrowded bunks. Elie Wiesel is in the second row of bunks, seventh from the left, next to the vertical beam.

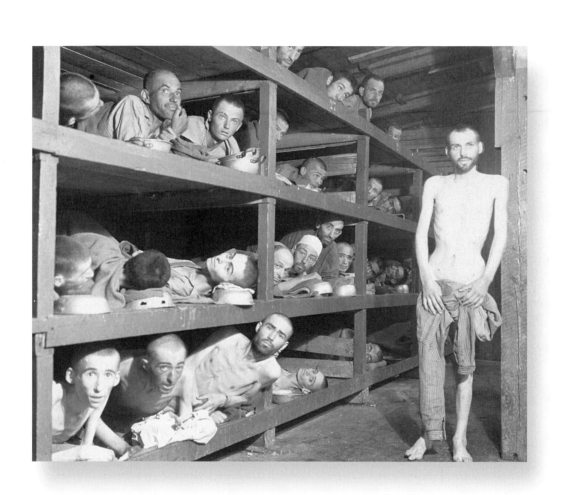

evening, he shared his soup with his father. Every day, Shlomo's eyes grew dimmer. His body was racked with dysentery. He refused food but wanted more and more water. Only water. He lay deathly sick for a week.

Soon, Shlomo Wiesel began to lose his mind. He cried out so often and so loudly that an officer hit him in the head with a stick. Elie has never forgotten his father's bloodstained face and battered skull.

On January 28, 1945, Wiesel went to sleep with his father in the bunk below him. "Eliezer," was the last word he heard his father say.[7] When he woke, another prisoner was in the bunk below him. His father was gone.

Food

After his father's death, Wiesel slipped into "a state of non-being."[8] He no longer feared beatings or death. He no longer felt hunger or thirst or fatigue. Sometimes, he did not even line up for bread or soup. He spent whole days in a state of dreamless sleep. He lost all desire to live . . . and yet, he lived. "As long as my father was alive, I was alive. When he died, I was no longer alive. It wasn't life; it was something else. I existed, but I did not live."[9]

Elie was in a daze. The Nazis transferred him to the children's block, and his hunger returned. All he thought of was food. All he dreamed of was soup. On April 5, things changed. The SS were late for the daily roll call. Hundreds of children waited for two hours. After that long wait, the SS announced that this was the end: no more bread, no more water, and no more soup. Every day, thousands of them would be killed in the crematories until there were simply none left. The Final Solution at last.

Six days later, on April 10, about twenty thousand starving prisoners gathered when the camp sirens went off. They waited for something to happen, but nothing did. Many slept. At 10:00 in the morning, members of a prisoners' resistance movement actually took over the camp. There was not a fight. The SS ran away. A silence fell over the prisoners, for no one knew what to do next.

The next day, the first American tank entered Buchenwald. American soldiers found about four hundred children left alive. Elie Wiesel was one of them.

> I will never forget the American soldiers and the horror that could be read in their faces. I will especially remember one black sergeant, a muscled giant, who wept tears of omnipotent rage and shame, shame for the human species, when he saw us.[10]

The soldiers tossed the children cans of food. Wiesel caught a can of what looked like ham or pork. He opened it, smelled it, and collapsed. Three days later, he lay in a hospital, hovering semiconsciously between life and death. Of the twenty thousand liberated prisoners, five thousand more died in the first days, mainly from "blood poisoning."[11] The rich food offered by well-intentioned American liberators caused deadly reactions in their emaciated bodies.

When he woke up, Wiesel summoned his strength to rise. *Night* ends with this famous image: "I wanted to see myself in the mirror hanging on the opposite wall. I had not seen myself since the ghetto. From the depths of the mirror, a corpse gazed back at me. The look in his eyes, as they stared into mine, has never left me."[12]

6

Wandering

As the Americans took charge of Buchenwald, they did the best they could to keep the former prisoners alive. Food, relief, and rescue workers poured in from all over the world. Although hundreds continued to die from disease and starvation, many liberated prisoners slowly began to regain their health and strength.

The new camp administrators had difficult decisions to make, and the decisions about children were the most challenging. Where would the orphans go? Back home to places like Sighet? What would be the point? Their parents and families were most likely dead, or if not, probably impossible to find. Europe was in postwar chaos. Perhaps the children could go to Palestine, the symbolic homeland of the Jews. However, the British, who governed Palestine in 1945, did not want refugees pouring in.

One day, Wiesel and the rest of the children of Buchenwald learned that about half of them would go to France; others would go to Great Britain and Switzerland. On June 2, 1945, representatives of a French children's rescue society, the *Oeuvre de Secours aux Enfants* (OSE), came to Buchenwald to escort a group of nearly five hundred children to France. Elie Wiesel was part of this group.

The children walked from Buchenwald to the train, but this time, they boarded comfortable passenger cars. As the train pulled away, Wiesel did not look back. Instead, he studied the countryside as they headed west. It was beginning to turn green. After three days, the train stopped and they disembarked. A man delivered a speech in French, but Wiesel could not understand a word. Many of the children raised their hands. Wiesel did not. He later found out that the man had asked who among the children wanted to become French citizens. He had missed his chance, a detail that would haunt him for years.

French peasants offered them bread, fruit, and cookies as they passed through villages and towns. On June 6, they reached Écouis, where they were greeted by other members of the OSE. Their mission was to care for the orphaned children until they could be independent. The OSE offered medical exams, clothing, shelter, and an abundance of food. They had expected very young children, but most of those who arrived were teenagers. Many boys were very angry at what had happened; some fought and behaved aggressively. But others, like Wiesel, drew inward; he began to keep a private journal.

After a few weeks, the staff of the orphanage divided the teenagers into two groups: those who wanted to practice Judaism and those who did not. Wiesel became part of the group who requested kosher food and prayer books. He picked up his study of the Talmud exactly where he had left

off in Sighet. "Immediately I plunged into study—and Jewish practice at the same time. I became as religious as before . . . Tradition gives an anchor, and I needed an anchor . . . I wanted to continue on the exact page of the book that I had abandoned when they took me away."[1]

Instead of feeling rage because of his experience, Wiesel felt gratitude. He said thank you to everyone he met, everyone who extended him even the smallest kindness.[2] He spent his days studying, hiking in the woods, talking, and taking French lessons. He also played a lot of chess. One day, someone took photographs of him as he played. He heard that the photographers were journalists.

A few days later, the director of the school told Wiesel that his sister Hilda had telephoned from Paris. She had recognized him in a photograph of chess players published in a newspaper and had immediately contacted the school. On his own, Wiesel took a train to Paris where Hilda met him with her husband Freddo, an Algerian Jew. They had met after the liberation and had fallen in love. Hilda told her brother that Bea had also survived and had returned to Sighet to find her brother, but it would be months before they would meet.

Some of the orphans went to Palestine to join family. Some went to school in Paris and to private homes. Wiesel was part of a group of ninety religious boys who moved to the estate of Dr. Charly Merzbadh, the Chateau d'Ambloy in Vaucelles, for the rest of the summer. There, they ate kosher food and studied all day, then enjoyed campfires and singing at night.

Escorted by American soldiers, children of Buchenwald file out of the main gate. Elie Wiesel is the fourth child in the left column.

In September 1946, they celebrated the Jewish New Year with special services. As they prayed Kaddish, the Jewish prayer for the dead, Wiesel wept hard for the first time.

Soon, the OSE moved them closer to Paris, and Wiesel found two teachers who would change his life. The first, François Wahl, was only two years older than Wiesel, but taught him to speak French. The second, a Talmudic scholar named Shushani, taught him about the mysteries of Judaism, history, and life. Shushani reminded Wiesel of Moché, his beloved teacher from Sighet. Wiesel often saw Hilda and weekly wrote to Bea. Bea was in a Displaced Persons camp near Kassel in the American zone of occupied Germany. By mid-1947, about two-hundred-fifty thousand homeless Jews lived in these camps that had been set up by the United Nations and the Allied armies. Wiesel visited Bea there two or three times. Each trip was difficult because of his lack of citizenship. He had no official papers. (To this day, he is afraid of police.)

At eighteen, Wiesel moved to a small studio apartment of his own. He continued to study, dreamed of going to Palestine, and directed a choir. He was painfully shy, and yet he became infatuated with nearly every young woman who crossed his path. He was still serious, intense, and driven, just as he was in Sighet. "I was considered bizarre, not to mention boring," he admits in his memoirs.[3] He could talk about philosophy, immortality, infinity, and God, but not really about everyday life.

For months, Wiesel studied and studied. He became attached to his friends and teachers and did not want to leave France. He faced the question of what to do with his life and thought that he might become a writer. He had always dreamed of writing. Perhaps he would write about what had happened in the camps—but could he?

Not yet. The words frightened him. *Genocide. God. Horror. Holocaust.* They all seemed trite and anemic. Elie Wiesel vowed not to write about his experiences for ten years: "Long enough to see clearly. Long enough to learn to listen to the voices crying inside my own. Long enough to regain possession of my memory. Long enough to unite the language of man with the silence of the dead."[4]

With the help of François Wahl, Wiesel enrolled in the Sorbonne, the University of Paris. While he was a student, his only income was a check from the OSE. From them, he received eight thousand francs each month (about sixteen dollars today). He constantly worried about money. Often, he only ate two meals a week.

At times, Wiesel was nearly overcome with the fear of failure and of not being able to support himself. He also felt a significant fear of women. He imagined suicide. He spent months in depression, often sick, studying his own face in the mirror, wondering about the direction of his young life. He kept his past locked inside. He was completely unsure of his future. He was alone, sad, and afraid.

As winter approached in 1947, an international event changed the course of Wiesel's life. Two thousand years ago, the Romans occupied the land of Israel and drove out most of the Jews. Jews settled in other countries around the world; their songs and tales mourn the loss of their homeland. This scattering of the Jews is called the Diaspora; Jews also call it Galut, meaning "the exile." On November 29, soon after Wiesel turned nineteen, the United Nations passed a resolution that granted Jews the right to a sovereign independent state. This was an essential step in establishing the new state of Israel.

This news inspired Elie Wiesel to take action. He discovered an underground Yiddish weekly newspaper called *Zion in Kamf*, wrote to its editor, and was offered a job.

A Job!

Wiesel was ecstatic. He would make 30,000 francs a month (about $60) and that salary would pay his bills. He moved to a new room—with a sink. At first, he translated French and Yiddish and began a crash course in language and writing—two passions he practices today. Soon, he was choosing stories and headlines, and attending press conferences and public demonstrations.

All the while, tensions mounted in the British Mandate in Palestine as Jews struggled against the British for the right to their homeland. Wiesel and his friend Nicolas signed up to join the Jewish underground army with many other eager volunteers. During the medical examination, a doctor told him that he could not be a soldier, for he was not in good health. The camps had taken their toll.

On May 14, 1948, David Ben-Gurion, the new prime minister, publicly read the Declaration of Independence of the State of Israel. Now, all Jews would have a homeland. On May 15, the new State of Israel became a nation of the world. A week later, Wiesel's first piece of writing appeared in *Zion in Kamf*, a tragic tale of two Jewish brothers fighting on opposing sides in Israel. He wrote it under the name Ben Shlomo (son of Shlomo).

Within a year, however, the radical newspaper folded and Wiesel was unemployed again.

Hilda and Bea

After the war, Wiesel's sister Hilda went to Paris with her husband, Freddo, an artist. Wiesel visited Hilda and Freddo in

Paris where they lived in a small apartment and struggled to get by. At least once, Uncle Eliezer baby-sat for his sister's son Sidney.

Bea's experiences in the death camps left her with damaged lungs, a disability that made it difficult for her to obtain a visa. For several years, she stayed in a Displaced Persons camp. While she waited, she worked for the United Nations administration as an executive secretary. Like her father, she was an outgoing organizer who had a gift for helping people. In 1949, she was granted permission to go to Canada. She settled in Montreal where she worked as a housekeeper for a Jewish family. Later, she worked with the Israeli consulate. During the next years, Wiesel visited his sister several times in Montreal, but they never talked about the past, a silence her brother would later regret.

The World Opens Up

Still in Paris, with a lot of time on his hands—especially at night—Wiesel began to read voraciously. He discovered the novels of the French writers François Mauriac, Jean Paul Sartre, and Albert Camus; the Spanish Miguel de Cervantes; the Austrian-Czech Franz Kafka, and the American William Faulkner. He accepted a few translating and editing jobs to pay the rent. Bea left for Canada; Hilda and Freddo were struggling financially; Shushani had disappeared. In the spring of 1949, Wiesel decided to go to Israel. For the first time in his life, Elie Wiesel left Europe.

Wiesel and several companions drove south through France to Marseilles. As they passed through a tunnel, a friend told him to close his eyes. When he opened them, he saw the ocean for the first time. The friends boarded the ship *Negba*, which would carry them to Israel. On board, one starry night, Wiesel experienced "a sadness . . . so powerful that I had a sudden urge to end my life, to throw myself overboard and be swallowed up and carried off by the waves."[5] A stranger spoke to him at that moment and probably saved his life.

Wiesel discovered Israel as a foreign correspondent who interviewed people and studied the politics of the new nation. What he found depressed him: People who already lived in Israel resented the new immigrants from Europe. He worked for a few weeks as a counselor in a children's home, but by autumn, he was ready to return to France. He arrived in Paris in January 1950, and soon made a vow of discipline: He would study no less than one hour a day for the rest of his life. He has kept it.

During his twenties, Wiesel wrote for magazines and newspapers. He wrote theater and concert reviews and articles on current events and local politics. He made a second trip from Paris to Israel and an automobile trip to Morocco. In Spain, he visited Madrid, Toledo, Saragossa, and Tangiers. He even made a short trip to Germany. Soon, he was offered a bi-monthly column in an Israeli daily newspaper called *Yedioth Ahronoth.* His column would be called "Sparks from the City of Light," which featured gossip and stories from the world of arts and letters.

In addition, Wiesel was offered a new kind of job: translating speeches from French to Yiddish during the World Jewish Conference in Geneva, Switzerland—for $200 a day. Those attending the conference would consider a proposal that Germany pay monetary compensation for 6 million Jewish deaths. Wiesel leapt at the chance to translate and be witness to the proceedings.

Still writing for newspapers and journals, Wiesel covered events in both Southeast Asia and the Soviet Union, where anti-Semitism was still very strong. He also wrote Hebrew subtitles for films.

In 1952, Wiesel won a lottery and used the money to travel to a completely different part of the world. He went to India, which had become independent from British rule in 1947. There, he learned to speak English and began writing a dissertation that he would never complete (comparing the fundamentals of Judaism, Christianity, and Hinduism). Although he was revolted by India's rigidly stratified caste system, he was drawn to the country's powerful spiritual forces. However, for him, the culture was *too* foreign to understand. He returned to France "even more Jewish than before."[6]

With France still his base, Wiesel went to Brazil in 1954 for *Yedioth Ahronoth*. On the long journey across the Atlantic by ship, he could not contain the words any longer. He wrote about the deportations, the camps, his father's death, and the liberation. He wrote about the loss of his childhood and his faith. During weeks at sea, he typed hundreds of pages in Yiddish in a kind of feverish trance. He did not even read what he wrote. When he finished, he had written over eight hundred pages. "It was impossible to write, but impossible not to write."[7]

In Brazil, while he was working, Wiesel met an Argentinean book publisher. The publisher asked about the manuscript Wiesel always carried with him. When Wiesel described it, the publisher asked for his only copy, promising to either return it or publish it. Wiesel gave it to him. The book was titled *Un die Velt Hot Geshvign (And the World Kept Silent)*.

Wiesel wrote *Un die Velt Hot Geshvign* in Yiddish, the language of his childhood. For him, Yiddish is the soul of Holocaust literature. "I know only one thing: if not for my first book, which I wrote in Yiddish, if not for my Yiddish memories, all my other books would have remained silent."[8]

Two months later, Wiesel returned to France energized and committed. He worked hard, studied, and made friends as the ten-year anniversary of his liberation from Buchenwald concentration camp neared.

The Interview

One evening in 1955, at an Independence Day celebration at the Israeli embassy in Paris, Wiesel spotted the famous writer François Mauriac. Two years earlier, Mauriac had won the Nobel Prize for Literature, the highest public honor a writer can achieve. Always the good journalist seeking a marketable story, Wiesel approached Mauriac in the hopes of exchanging a word or two. As Wiesel helped Mauriac on with his coat, he asked for an interview. To the young reporter's great surprise, the famous writer pulled out his calendar and scheduled one.

On the day of their meeting, Wiesel arrived an hour early, pacing up and down the street outside Mauriac's elegant home. Inside, he was greeted by a housekeeper and led to the living room. Mauriac quickly put the young reporter at ease as he spoke about Paris politics. Soon, the interview turned to one of Mauriac's favorite subjects: Jesus. As the seventy year old spoke of Jesus' suffering and death, the young Elie Wiesel grew more and more distressed. Finally, Wiesel closed his notebook and challenged Mauriac, recalling the 6 million Jewish people who died during the Holocaust, and yet, "we don't speak about them."[9] Trembling, Wiesel turned and headed for the elevator.

Mauriac followed him, caught up to him in the hallway, and gently touched his arm, asking him to return. Back in his office, the old writer openly wept. Ashamed of the disrespect he had shown, Wiesel struggled to apologize, but Mauriac

François Mauriac (1885–1970)

Born in Bordeaux, France, François Mauriac was the youngest of five children. His father died when he was only eighteen months old. He grew up in a sheltered world, first at home with his mother, and then in a Catholic school. As a young adult, he studied literature in Bordeaux and Paris.

He achieved fame and fortune in 1922 with *Le Baiser Au Lepreux [A Kiss for the Leper]*. During World War II, he lived in Nazi-occupied France and continued to write and publish his work. In 1964, he completed a comprehensive study of Charles DeGaulle, French general and statesman and president from 1959 to 1969.

Mauriac, considered one of France's literary masters, is best known and admired for his novels. His main characters struggle with crime, deceit, and the dark side of life and themselves. Among the most famous are *Le Desert de L'Amour [The Desert of Love]* (1925), and *Le Noeud de Viperes [The Knot of Vipers]* (1932).

In 1952, Mauriac won the Nobel Prize for Literature. His acceptance speech in Stockholm included these words: "The mystery of evil—there are no two ways of approaching it. We must either deny evil or we must accept it as it appears both within ourselves and without—in our individual lives, that of our passions, as well as in the history written with the blood of men by power-hungry empires."[10]

encouraged him to say more. The elder writer wanted to know everything about the death camps, but there was much that Wiesel still could not say. In the hallway, as he was leaving, Mauriac embraced Wiesel and said, "You are wrong not to speak . . . Listen to the old man that I am: one must speak out."[11]

New York City

Wiesel listened to the great writer who became, in some ways, a mentor. He revised the Yiddish version of his testimony into a much shorter French version and accepted Mauriac's help and advice. Even with Mauriac's support, it took many months for the book to be accepted for publication in France.

In the meantime, Wiesel made another trip to Israel. When he returned, the newspaper he worked for, *Yedioth Ahronoth*, asked him to go to New York City for a year. They would raise his salary to $160 a month. When Wiesel questioned his ability to live in New York on that amount, his editor suggested that giving speeches would bring more income. Wiesel agreed to go. In December 1955, before he said good-bye to Europe, he received his first copy of *Un die Velt Hot Geshvign* from Buenos Aires.

In New York City, Wiesel lived in four apartments before he finally found the right one in the Masters Hotel on Riverside Drive and 103rd Street. He would live there for the next thirteen years. It was a small studio with a sweeping view of Manhattan and the Hudson River. He spent a lot of his time looking out that window and writing.

Soon, the young reporter acquired a desk in the United Nations pressroom, and this opened up many professional doors. He did freelance writing for a Yiddish daily newspaper. He wrote a romantic spy novel (under the name Elisha

Carmeli) that was published as *Silent Heroes*. In it, all of the characters die.

In July 1956, Wiesel went with a friend, Aviva, to see a film. As they crossed Seventh Avenue at Forty-fifth Street, Wiesel was hit by a taxi. The impact threw him all the way to the next block. An ambulance took him to three different hospitals before they found one that would admit him. (His physical state seemed beyond repair; his wallet was empty; he had refugee papers; and he had no insurance.) At New York Hospital, in ten hours of surgery, Dr. Paul Braunstein repaired forty-seven fractures on his shattered left side. Elie Wiesel woke up, dazed and medicated, in a cast from head to foot.

7

Storyteller

The irony that he had survived Auschwitz but nearly died on a New York City street was not lost on Elie Wiesel. In fact, when he first emerged from his medication-induced coma, the whole situation seemed almost funny. His surgeon recognized meaning in Wiesel's survival: ". . . I don't think we could have lost Elie despite his terrible injuries because I believe in the wisdom of God. I truthfully believe that God had to have Elie to be the conscience of man [sic] about the Holocaust and about genocide."[1]

As Wiesel recovered, Aviva and Bea visited every day and colleagues met in his hospital room to discuss UN matters. One day, a lawyer representing the taxi company offered him a quarter of a million dollars to compensate for the accident, but his friends talked him out of it, claiming he could get more. Two years later, he settled for far less, just enough to pay his bills, pay the hospital, pay back the friend who loaned him money while he recovered—and pay the lawyer who handled his case.

Wiesel was confined to the hospital for weeks and then to a wheelchair for nearly a year. To this day, he has trouble walking or standing for more than ten minutes at a time, and he always sits when giving lectures. During his recovery, he chose the United States as his physical home and began the application process for citizenship from New York City.

Accepted

Also during his recovery, in 1957, Wiesel received word from François Mauriac that his testimony about the death camps had been accepted by Jérome Lindon, an editor at Editions de Minuit, a French publishing house. Lindon wanted to change the title to *La Nuit (Night)* and wanted to trim the manuscript even more. Wiesel had cut the original 864 pages to 245; Lindon edited it to 178. Mauriac himself wrote an eloquent introduction and praised the book to the press. *La Nuit* was hardly a best-seller, but reviews were favorable and Wiesel was interviewed on French television.

Soon after *La Nuit*'s publication, in 1958, Elie's sister Bea surprised her brother with the news of her engagement to Dr. Leonard Jackson in Montreal. In the years to follow, Bea and her husband had two children: Steve (who served as a military doctor in Israel in the 1990s, married, and fathered two) and Sarah, the mother of six.

Despite Mauriac's support and *Night*'s success in Europe, American publishers were not interested in Wiesel's testimony. Some thought it too short; others thought it too depressing. Others predicted Wiesel would be a "one book author." In 1960, Hill and Wang agreed to publish the first English edition and paid Wiesel an advance of $100. It sold only 1,046 copies in the first eighteen months.

Dedicated to Tzipora, his little sister who died at Auschwitz, *Night* is a simply-told tale, chilling in its brevity and the force of its first-person narrative. It is the product of an extreme distillation in which events speak for themselves. The tone is even but hauntingly sad. It is a story of initiation during which the narrator faces death—of a mother, a little sister, a father, and an entire community of family, teachers, and friends.

The first chapter of *Night* takes place in Sighet in 1941, with Moché and the grocery store and the family on Serpent Street. The last chapter ends soon after the liberation of Buchenwald in April 1945. Today, *Night* is the world's most widely read piece of Holocaust testimony. Since 1958, it has been translated into thirty languages, and it has sold more than 5 million copies throughout the world. Many people born after World War II are introduced to the Holocaust by reading *Night*. Every year, Wiesel gets hundreds of letters from students who have read it. He answers each one, grateful that so many young readers are moved by his words. The income from it supports a school in Israel established by Wiesel in memory of his father.

Wiesel admits that *Night* is the foundation of all his work: "All the rest is commentary." Even Wiesel himself, however, writes with a storyteller's distance, for the real story defies language and can never be told. While *Night* is as close as he can come to the truth of the experience, it does not and cannot tell the tale. During a 1992 interview, Wiesel admitted, "To make [the Holocaust] understandable, we must *understate* it. That's why in this little book, *Night* . . . what I *don't* say is important, as important as the things I *do* say. But even if you read all the books, all the documents, by all the survivors, you still would not know."[2]

Onward from Night

In 1960, the same year that *Night* was published, Adolf Eichmann was captured in Argentina and put on trial in

Israel. Wiesel covered the trial as a reporter for the *Jewish Daily Forward*. Each day, he sat and listened to survivors' testimonies against the SS general who had run the death trains with heinous efficiency. Some of the survivors cried; others seemed dazed; still others spoke in clear, strong voices. Three judges listened intently. Eichmann seemed "utterly unmoved" by the chilling testimonies. Wiesel stared at Eichmann for hours, frightened by how ordinary a man he seemed. "It irritated me to think of Eichmann as human. I would have preferred him to have a monstrous countenance, like a Picasso portrait with three ears and four eyes."[3] Eichmann was found guilty and executed in 1962.

Wiesel's second book, *Dawn* (1961), is a novel, and not an autobiography; that is, it is fiction not nonfiction. Dedicated to François Mauriac, *Dawn* tells the tale of an eighteen-year-old member of the Jewish underground in Palestine (and a Holocaust survivor) named Elisha. Ordered to shoot a British hostage at dawn, Elisha faces the moral dilemma of whether the killing is justified. Here, Wiesel begins a practice he uses in all of his novels: using personal experience as the basis for literary fiction. For example, in his third book, *Le Jour* (which means "the day" in French), published in English as *The Accident* in 1962, the main character attempts suicide by stepping in front of a taxi. Wiesel dedicated *The Accident* to his surgeon, Dr. Paul Braunstein.

By the early 1960s, Wiesel's books were selling well enough to pay his bills. When Arthur Wang, publisher of *Night*, *Dawn*, and *The Accident*, advised him to take his fourth book, *The Town Beyond the Wall* (1964), to a larger publishing house (Antheneum), Wiesel began to work with different publishers. In all, Elie Wiesel has authored over fifty books.

They include novels, essays, plays, memoirs, legends, interviews, conversations, and even lyrics.

Twelve of Wiesel's books are novels. The first five, written from 1960 to 1968, are seen by literary critics as a cumulative journey. Each of the protagonists is a male Holocaust survivor, but none are exactly like Wiesel himself. Each of the first five novels poses a different moral dilemma and explores a possible reaction to the Holocaust. *Dawn* is about political action. *The Accident* explores suicide. *The Town Beyond the Wall* is about madness; *Gates of the Forest*, about friendship. *A Beggar in Jerusalem*, a fictional account of the Six-Day War between Israel and its Arab neighbors, is about the cycles of history. According to the literary critics who have analyzed them, the five novels represent movement from darkness to light, from self-absorption to social awareness, and from solitude to community.[4]

Wiesel wrote *Night* in Yiddish, the language of his childhood. He wrote all the other books in French, but most have been translated into English and other languages. Wiesel claims not to know English well and admits that, after the war, he needed a new language in the same way that he needed a new home. French—and France—were there for him. When Elie Wiesel became a United States citizen in 1963, he claimed another home. "The day I received American citizenship was a turning point in my life. I had ceased to be stateless. Until then, unprotected by any government and unwanted by any society, the Jew in me was overcome by a feeling of pride mixed with gratitude."[5]

A Partner

Many writers wonder if Israel is yet another home to Elie Wiesel. It *is* where he chose to be married.

In the mid-1960s, friends introduced Wiesel, then nearly forty, to a young mother in the midst of a divorce. The two had lunch together; she talked, he listened. She too had spent the war in Europe, moving from place to place to evade the Nazis. She had a twelve-year-old daughter, Jennifer. She was fluent in five languages and commanded a broad knowledge of theater, art, and music. Her name was Marion Rose.

On April 2, 1969, in the Old City of Jerusalem, the ancient synagogue, the Ramban, was opened for the wedding of Eliezer Wiesel to Marion Rose. It was the eve of Passover. Wiesel's sisters, Bea and Hilda, attended with their families, along with a few cousins and many friends. During the ceremony, Wiesel missed his mother and father so much he had trouble concentrating. Afterwards, during singing and feasting, he sobbed. The newlyweds spent their wedding night at the King David Hotel overlooking the Old City.

Since that day, Marion has been at Wiesel's side. In the time they have been together, she has translated most of her husband's books from French to English. Dedicated to Marion, the 1970 novel *A Beggar in Jerusalem* sold over ten thousand copies and won the Prix Médicis, a prestigious European literary award. "I do nothing without asking her advice," Wiesel admits today.[6]

A Man of Many Voices

Soon, Wiesel began to experiment with other kinds of writing. For example, *One Generation After* (1970) begins with World War II and ends with the Israeli Six-Day War in 1967, but it braids three kinds of writing together. In it are Hasidic legends, stark dialogues between characters both imagined and real, and passages of candid autobiography.

Several other books are collections of essays. The first of these was written after Wiesel traveled to the Soviet Union

Marion Erster Rose Wiesel (b. 1932)

In 1940, the Nazis entered Belgium, and the Rose family fled to France where they landed in an internment camp. "The basic difference between these and concentration camps is that there was no organized extermination. They let you die of hunger and diseases," Marion Wiesel says.[7] Marion Rose came to the United States in 1949.

Many years later, after Marion Rose became Marion Wiesel, she edited a book of photographs by Roman Vishniac of Jewish life in Eastern Europe before the war: *To Give Them Light.* Later, Arthur Cohn asked her to write an HBO film about the 1.5 million children murdered in the Holocaust. "I didn't think a factual approach would work," Marion Wiesel said. "To me, what was important was to shine the light on their faces—to make people feel that it could have been them, that it could happen again and that everybody is vulnerable."[8] The haunting eighteen-minute *Children of the Night* consists of footage of children in ghettos and on their way to the camps.

Today, Marion Wiesel works for the Elie Wiesel Foundation for Humanity. Its mission is to combat indifference, intolerance, and injustice all over the world by creating forums for the discussion and resolution of urgent ethical issues.

In 2001, President Clinton presented Marion Wiesel with the Presidential Citizens Medal for her "mission of hope against hate, of life against death, of good over evil."[9]

in 1965 and again in 1966. During these trips, he interviewed hundreds of Russian Jews in Moscow, Leningrad, Kiev, and Tbilisi. "I returned transformed," he writes in his memoirs. *The Jews of Silence* (1966), originally a series of articles written for *Yedioth Ahronoth*, describes a Jewish community living in fear. The book sparked American interest in Soviet Jews and furthered the rights of Soviet Jews to emigrate, especially to the United States and Israel.

Legends of Our Time (1968) contains fifteen essays on subjects such as his father's death, his teachers, and Moché the "madman" from Sighet. *A Jew Today* (1978) contains portraits, letters, essays, and again, spare dialogues that capture intimate, but totally imagined, conversations. One is between a father and his son. In another titled "A Man and His Little Sister" Wiesel talks with Tzipora.

By the 1970s, Wiesel was "looking for a different way to express myself."[10] In 1973, he wrote the words of a cantata that Darius Milhaud set to music. *Ani Maamin (I Believe)* was first performed at Carnegie Hall in New York City on November 11, 1973. The words are based on a playful, traditional song that prisoners sang in Auschwitz. In the cantata, Abraham, Isaac, and Jacob appeal to a silent God. In 1974, Wiesel wrote the first of his two plays. In *Zalmen, or the Madness of God*, a lowly Russian madman scolds an old rabbi for remaining silent. The rabbi suddenly speaks like a Biblical prophet in a mystical frenzy. *Zalmen* was performed in many theaters in Europe and the United States.

During these experimental years, Wiesel also found a voice as a vibrant and popular university professor. From 1972 to 1976, he served as professor of Judaic Studies at City University in New York City. There, he taught a popular class on the Holocaust, often to children of survivors. After short stints at Florida International University and Yale, he was appointed the Andrew W. Mellon Professor in the Humanities at Boston University and has taught there since 1976. He commutes from New York once a week in the fall to teach a class and advise graduate students in philosophy and theology. Students sign up a year in advance to take his courses, which he never teaches more than once. His courses have included "The Theme of Reconciliation in Ancient and Modern Philosophy and Literature," one devoted to the writings of Franz Kafka, and another that compared the greatest books by certain authors with their first books.

These years of prolific writing, teaching, and traveling were punctuated by yet another family loss. In 1974, after two years of illness, Wiesel's sister Bea died of lung cancer, at the age of forty-eight. In his memoirs, Wiesel expresses regret that he never spoke to Bea about her experiences in the camps. When Wiesel goes to Montreal, he visits Bea's grave and reads from a stone with many names: his sister's, of course, but also the names of family members who do not have gravestones of their own.

The Hasidic Tradition

Wiesel has authored a half dozen books that retell the stories of the great Jewish traditions, both Biblical and Hasidic. The first, *Souls on Fire* (1972), which Wiesel calls "the sum of my childhood,"[11] celebrates his beloved Hasidic teachers in tales, legends, parables, sayings, and personal reflections. *Messengers of God* (1976) retells the stories of the Biblical heroes Adam, Job, Jacob, Abraham, Joseph, and Moses. *Four Hasidic Masters* (1978) describes Pinhas of Koretz, Barukh of Medzebozh, the Holy Seer of Lublin, and Naphtali of Ropshitz, four Eastern European Hassidic Rebbes from the eighteenth and nineteenth centuries.

In 1976, Wiesel began a series of lectures at the Ninety-second Street YM-YWHA (Young Men's-Young Women's Hebrew Association) in New York City—four lectures a year to packed houses. People still clamor to hear his voice tell musical stories that reveal timeless truths. Sometimes, his voice is very sad and quiet; other times, he is dramatic and angry. In these lectures, Wiesel explores Hasidic teachings through a series of portraits of the movement's founders. In 1991, he published *Sages and Dreamers* based on these lectures. He still offers free public lectures each fall at Boston University.

The Center Point

Wiesel admits that the main obsession in his life is *how to transmit.* The difference between life and death for Wiesel is that life transmits and death stops. If a person cannot transmit, that person is dead. Wiesel uses words to do this, both spoken and written. He also writes to correct injustices. For example, when an entire community is killed, it might also be forgotten . . . unless someone remembers that community and writes about it for others to read. Then, he feels, some justice is done. He writes to prevent his own madness. He writes to communicate visions. And finally, and most importantly perhaps, he writes to bear witness to all those Jewish deaths, to "wrest those victims from oblivion. To help the dead vanquish death."[12]

During this period of his life, Wiesel wrote for four hours every day, except Shabbat and Jewish holidays. He spent another four hours reading and studying. He kept fiction and nonfiction projects on his desk at the same time. "I'm a compulsive worker," he admitted. "I work sixteen hours a day. I don't sleep much."[13] While he writes, he listens to music, usually classical. Wiesel does not drink alcohol and is somewhat indifferent to food—except chocolate, which he loves.

In a 1978 interview, Wiesel said that he writes every book three times. The first draft is usually quite long. He puts it away. Weeks later, he writes another draft without looking at the first one. Finally, the third draft combines elements of the first two drafts, but it is always much shorter. Revision involves cutting, paring language to its essentials.

For Elie Wiesel, every book has its own melody. Once he discovers it, the book takes off. He is not always sure where the book is headed, but he finds out as he writes: ". . . suddenly, at the corner of a sentence, an astonishing discovery; *this* is where I was trying to go."[14] When an interviewer once asked about writer's block, Wiesel's answer was simple: "I have never felt blocked."[15] However, he does admit to writing very slowly. "I write in a sort of anguished pleasure. Or a pleasurable anguish? There is much of both in my writing, and even in the process of writing."[16]

In all of his writing—novels, tales, essays, speeches, letters—Elie Wiesel asks questions. His central characters ask questions; his essays often begin or end with questions; the speakers in his Hasidic tales are questioners, seekers, and visionaries. "What does it all mean?" they all seem to be asking. "What does it mean to be a human being living in the world today?" He describes all of his work as a question mark.[17]

Wiesel is not only a prolific writer but also an avid reader who reads in French. His office is full of books, stacks of them everywhere, walls lined with bookcases. He tries to read everything that appears on the subjects of World War II and the Holocaust.

According to Wiesel, all his stories are one story. He pictures them as concentric circles. Their centers are the same point: his experience in the camps when he was fifteen years old. Ironically, this center is a place and time that words can never express. The center point for Elie Wiesel is silence.

The Cultural Conscience

During the 1950s and 1960s, most Americans avoided the topic of the Holocaust. They did not want to be reminded of the death camps. Nor did they want to consider their own responsibility for their country's indifference. As the world rebuilt itself after World War II, new alliances were forged, sometimes among old enemies; and new enemies were made, sometimes among old friends. For example, West Germany became a United States ally in the "cold war" against the Soviet Union.

Three things happened, however, to challenge this cultural denial. The first was the 1967 Israeli victory over Egypt, Syria, Jordan, and Iraq in the Six-Day War. The fortitude of the new Jewish nation and the quick and resounding victory of the Israeli Army caught the attention of the whole world. Secondly, during the Vietnam War, especially after the massacre of civilians at My Lai, people began to remember the atrocities of the Holocaust and draw comparisons. During the turbulent 1960s, universities began teaching courses on the Holocaust as more and more people questioned America's role in Vietnam and its commitment to basic human rights. Thirdly, in April 1978, NBC aired a four-part miniseries entitled *Holocaust*.

Elie Wiesel reviewed the miniseries for the *New York Times*. Foremost, he faulted the producers for calling it a documentary when, in fact, it was fiction. He criticized the scope of the film as too broad and all-inclusive to be historically accurate. He was appalled that NBC did not hire a single survivor as a consultant for the production. He also cited errors, such as a rabbi reciting the wrong blessing during a wedding. His review ends, "The Holocaust *must* be remembered. But not as a show."[18] Despite these criticisms, the miniseries exposed 120 million people to this chapter in history, and many were learning about it for the first time.

Days after *Holocaust* aired, President Jimmy Carter announced the formation of the President's Commission on the Holocaust. He nominated Elie Wiesel as the chairperson of the fifteen-member commission.

Wiesel's first reaction was to say no. He was a writer, not a political organizer. Others argued, however, that he was the best person for this job. His closest advisors convinced him that this was an opportunity for remembrance on a grand scale. Plus, American Jews trusted him because he had been there—and survived.

President Carter met with Wiesel. Together, they looked at CIA aerial photographs of Auschwitz taken by American bombers in 1944. The photos showed the crematory chimneys and the blocks. Wiesel could see where he and his father had lived. Together, Carter and Wiesel wondered why the Allies never bombed the death camps—or at least the railroads that led to them. Neither had an answer. What could be done now? Remembrance.

Wiesel accepted the nomination to become chairperson of the commission. On February 15, 1979, House Speaker Thomas (Tip) O'Neill swore Wiesel into his new office.

A Son

On June 6, 1972, at age forty-three, Elie Wiesel became a father. He and Marion named their son Elisha (Shlomo ben Eliezer). The event changed Elie Wiesel's life, and yet, intensely private, he avoids speaking or writing much about his only son. This dimension of Wiesel's humanity, however, is testimony to his faith in the future of the Jewish people: "It was Marion who persuaded me [to have a child]. It was wrong to give the killers one more victory. The long line from which I sprang must not end with me. She was right. And now? Because of my father and my son, I choose commitment."[19]

Father and son in their New York City home, in 1982.

93

The birth of a son marked a new center point of Wiesel's life. "It will mark my existence forever. This little fellow in the arms of his mother will illuminate our life. I look at him and look at him. And as I look at him I feel the presence of others also seeking to protect him."[20] Suddenly, he had a new role: protector. "My son changed me. Once you bring life into the world, you must protect it. We must protect it by changing the world."[21]

When Elisha was two, Wiesel bragged that his son's favorite toy was a typewriter. When Elisha was a child, Wiesel called him every day, no matter where he was, and took him along on trips that lasted longer than a week. When Elisha was six, he noticed A-7713 on his father's arm and asked what it was. His father was speechless. After Wiesel finally answered, a flood of questions ensued, "Did wicked people do it? Why don't I have a grandfather? Was it like Pharaoh in Egypt, who wanted to kill all the Jews?"[22]

In time, Wiesel would teach his son the answers to these questions. He would also continue to teach the world.

8

Conscience

The first meeting of the new commission took place on February 15, 1979. In the following months, the group traveled to Poland and visited Warsaw, Krakow, and Auschwitz. It was Wiesel's first return to the site of the death camp. In his memoirs, he writes of the profound silence of the place. The loudest sounds were his own memories of barking dogs, screaming men. "The watchtowers. The barbed wire." He describes it as a haunting experience and writes about it as "a cursed place." In his memoirs, he recalls his first visit there in the summer of 1979.

> As I return to Birkenau, centuries after leaving it, I leave reality behind and find myself face to face with the adolescent I was then. Only now it all seems calm, almost peaceful. I close my eyes, and from the depths of time, hallucinating images appear. The thick smoke, the small heaps of ashes. Blank-faced men running in all directions. In Birkenau, no one moved slowly, especially not Death, which after all must be everywhere at once.[1]

Members of the commission also traveled to Kiev and then on to Moscow. By September, the commission offered a formal written report to President Carter. In it, they made five recommendations:

1. Create a "living museum" in the United States with spiritual and education components
2. Recognize annual Days of Remembrance to honor the victims of the Holocaust
3. Ratify the Genocide Treaty, an international treaty that places genocide outside any law
4. Put pressure on foreign countries to prosecute Nazi war criminals and to care for Jewish cemeteries
5. Create a United States Holocaust Memorial Council to implement these actions

Here is the beginning of the commission's report, authored by Wiesel:

> It is with a deep sense of privilege that I submit to you, in accordance with your request, the report of your Commission on the Holocaust. Never before have its members, individually and collectively, given so much of themselves to a task that is both awesome and forbidding, a task which required reaching far back into the past as well as taking a hard look into the future.
>
> Our central focus was memory—our own and that of the victims during a time of unprecedented evil and suffering. That was the Holocaust, an era we must remember not only because of the dead; it is too late for them. Not only because of the survivors; it may even be late for them. Our remembering is an act of generosity, aimed at saving men and women from apathy to evil, if not from evil itself.
>
> We wish, through the work of this Commission, to reach and transform as many human beings as possible. We hope to share our conviction that when war and

genocide unleash hatred against any one people or peoples, all are ultimately engulfed in the fire.

With this conviction and mindful of your mandate, Mr. President, we have explored during the past several months of our existence the various ways and means of remembering— and of moving others to remember—the Holocaust and its victims, an event that was intended to erase memory.

Our first question may sound rhetorical: Why remember, why remember at all? Is not human nature opposed to keeping alive memories that hurt and disturb? The more cruel the wound, the greater the effort to cover it, to hide it beneath other wounds, other scars. Why then cling to unbearable memories that may forever rob us of our sleep? Why not forget, turn the page, and proclaim: let it remain buried beneath the dark nightmares of our subconscious. Why not spare our children the weight of our collective burden and allow them to start their lives free of nocturnal obsessions and complexes, free of Auschwitz and its shadows?

These questions, Mr. President, would not perhaps be devoid of merit if it were possible to extirpate the Holocaust from history and make believe we can forget. But it is not possible and we cannot. Like it or not, the Event must and will dominate future events. Its centrality in the creative endeavors of our contemporaries remains undisputed. Philosophers and social scientists, psychologists and moralists, theologians and artists: all have termed it a watershed in the annals of mankind. What was comprehensible before Treblinka[2] is comprehensible no longer. After Treblinka, man's ability to cope with his condition was shattered; he was pushed to his limits and beyond. Whatever has happened since must therefore be judged in the light of Treblinka. Forgetfulness is no solution.[3]

Throughout his long life, Wiesel has stayed true to his deepest beliefs. One of these is that one cannot remember the Holocaust without remembering that it was a *Jewish* tragedy, first and foremost. Although he acknowledges that others—Poles, Gypsies, Soviet prisoners of war, homosexuals, Jehovah's Witnesses, the mentally ill—were killed in the death camps, Jews died in incomparable numbers. Of the 11 million victims of the Nazis, 6 million were Jews. Wiesel consistently reminds the world to include the word "Jew" when we speak or write about the Holocaust.

> During our journey to Eastern Europe . . . the Commission observed that while Jews are sometimes mentioned on public monuments in Poland, they were not referred to in Russia at all. In Kiev's Babi Yar, for instance, where nearly 80,000 Jews were murdered in September 1941, the word Jew is totally absent from the memorial inscriptions. Our Commission believes that because they were the principal target of Hitler's Final Solution, we must remember the six million Jews and, through them and beyond them, but never without them, rescue from oblivion all the men, women and children, Jewish and non-Jewish, who perished in those years in the forests and camps of the kingdom of night.[4]

Wiesel is outspoken and passionate on this subject, but not everyone agrees, not even all Jews. For example, Simon Wiesenthal, the famous Nazi-hunter, reminds everyone that Jews were not the only victims of the Nazis; he has criticized Wiesel for being too narrowly focused.

A year later, Wiesel was appointed chairperson of the newly created United States Holocaust Memorial Council, whose work began with defining its own membership—and began with disagreements, mostly over politics and personalities. In the end, the council had sixty-five members. Many were political appointees; many were not even Jewish; and ten were members of Congress.

Wiesel's first action as the chairperson of the council was to summarize its purpose in a single sentence: "For the dead *and* the living, we must bear witness." Today, this purpose is engraved on the wall of the United States Holocaust Memorial Museum.

Three months after it was organized, the council held its first Day of Remembrance on April 24, 1979. It was held in the Rotunda, the great hall of the Capitol of the United States. President Carter held Elisha, Wiesel's son, on his knee for much of the program and then spoke with a great sense of history. This Ceremony of Remembrance is now an annual event, established by an Act of Congress. Each year, it takes place in Washington, D.C., and in all fifty state capitols. The date each year is based on the Jewish calendar, including the traditional period of mourning known as the Counting of the Omer.

Holocaust Days of Remembrance

Tuesday	April 25, 2006
Sunday	April 15, 2007
Thursday	May 1, 2008
Tuesday	April 21, 2009
Sunday	April 11, 2010
Sunday	May 1, 2011
Thursday	April 19, 2012
Sunday	April 7, 2013
Sunday	April 27, 2014

In the midst of all this emotion, travel, and political spotlight, Wiesel continued to write. He continued to experiment with form and to blend his story with stories from the past. As before, his writing reflects both inner turmoil—and yet, a willingness to chisel through moral and philosophical questions with the tools of words, reason, and imagination. In 1979, he published his second drama, *The Trial of God*. The play shows three seventeenth-century Ukrainian actors stage a mock trial of a God who kept silent in the face of evil.

Missions, Meetings, and a "Living Memorial"

In the 1980s, Wiesel's new role led him to travel all over the world. In 1980, he journeyed to Cambodia with an international group of humanitarians to protest the atrocities committed by Pol Pot and his Khmer Rouge. Their mission was to deliver food and medicine to refugees, victims of war and famine. The group was stopped at the border by guards. As they waited in silent protest, it was thirty-five years to the day that Shlomo had died in Buchenwald. Wiesel and other Jews prayed Kaddish for his father and for the Cambodians who were dying. A day later, the Red Cross distributed the supplies. In 1982, Wiesel went to Nicaragua to meet members of the Miskito tribe expelled from their home by Daniel Ortega's regime.

> He immediately flew . . . down to Honduras, took a little plane to get as close as he could. Then they got in a dugout canoe to get to the Miskito Indians, met with them, and flew back to issue his report. Without stopping, he got on a plane to Paris to speak to French government officials who were planning on selling helicopter gunships to the Sandinistas. He told them what was going on, and Mitterrand [President of France] canceled the helicopters.[5]

In 1985, Wiesel journeyed to South Africa to voice his opposition to apartheid, the policy of racial segregation of blacks from whites, and he participated in a conference to explore the possibility of political asylum for refugees from El Salvador and Guatemala.

The Days of Remembrance, established by the commission, have spawned international workshops and conferences that allow survivors, historians, artists, political leaders, and humanitarians to meet, discuss, share, and strategize about ways to remember the Holocaust and prevent it from happening again. For example, in 1981, Wiesel helped organize the International Liberators Conference in the State Department. The idea came from a meeting in Moscow with the Russian general who had liberated Auschwitz. "I suddenly had the idea of bringing together liberators from *all* the allied forces. To listen to you and to thank you. And—why not admit it?—to solicit your help. *Our* testimony is being disputed by morally deranged Nazis and Nazi-lovers; your voices may silence them."[6] In 1984, "The Courage to Care," a conference organized by Dr. Carol Rittner, celebrated the non-Jews who risked their lives to save Jews during the Holocaust. "Seventy-five guests, Jews and Christians, from diverse backgrounds arrive to take part in this gathering . . . We witness the reunions of several 'saviors' and those they saved. People are embracing, and there is much weeping in the corridors."[7] Other international conferences include the Holocaust Writers' Conference (1980), the World Gathering of Jewish Holocaust Survivors (1981; nearly seven thousand survivors and their families attended), the International Conference on Holocaust and Genocide (1982), and the Conference on Judaism, and War, and the Nuclear Arms Race (1986).

Wiesel loves the conferences because they spawn friendships and collaborations. They are living, breathing events during which people meet, discuss, debate, and learn. On the other hand, Wiesel made it clear to everyone that he would not support the building of a nonliving monument. Neither did he want a museum that was simply an exhibit. In 1980, the United States Congress authorized "a permanent living memorial" to all the victims of the Holocaust. Through the arduous process of planning, designing, locating, constructing, and filling the memorial, Wiesel discovered, somewhat sadly, that people defined "living memorial" in a variety of ways.

Hundreds of people built the United States Holocaust Memorial Museum, but the leadership of one man made it all happen. In the official history of the museum, the authors write, "It was Elie Wiesel whose vision, initiative, and power of persuasion led to the establishment of the Commission and the Council. His spirit inspired not only the Commission's recommendations but also the very process of creating the Museum. Were it not for him, the Museum would not have come into existence."[8]

Seeing the museum from idea to reality took ten years. The first phase was spent planning and fund-raising. In 1983, Wiesel was given the keys to a red brick building on the Mall in Washington, D.C., that had formerly housed the Auditor's Complex. Wiesel was pleased with the building that was, in his opinion, "appropriate because of its simplicity" and located on a "most prestigious site" close to the Lincoln Memorial.[9] After work began, renovators determined the building was so rotten inside that it was in danger of collapse. They would have to tear it down and build from the ground up.

In December 1984, the red brick building was razed with plans to build a new building on the same site. For a year, Wiesel's closest advisors disagreed over architects and designs. Architect James Ingo Freed wanted the museum to be a "resonator of memory" but like "permanent living memorial," the phrase held different meanings for different persons—all of them passionate. Their disagreements grew into antagonism and hostilities. As the months passed, Wiesel grew more and more frustrated with the process and burdened by an enormous sense of failure. "I am a poor manager, a bad administrator. I have problems giving orders, and I am incapable of hurting anyone, even in the name of supposedly sacred aims."[10] When he resigned as chairperson in 1986, the museum was still not built.

A Fast Pace

While the museum was planned and replanned, while Elisha attended elementary school, while he taught at Boston University, Elie Wiesel continued to write. The books from this period reflect his fascination with Jewish history, in particular, Jewish teachers and leaders. In 1981, he published *Five Biblical Portraits*, the Biblical tales of Joshua, Saul, Elijah, Jeremiah, and Jonah. In 1982, *Somewhere a Master* appeared. The book portrayed the disciples of the great Hasidic master Baal Shem Tov. In *The Golem* (1983), Wiesel collects centuries-old legends about a mythical clay creature who comes to life. Through it all, his passion for writing never wavered; his dedication to writing never waned, even when the world, and his teaching, pulled him in many directions.

A *Boston Magazine* article described a typical Monday for Elie Wiesel, Boston University professor. He rose at 5:00 A.M. and took the shuttle from New York City to Boston. By 8:15 he was seeing students in his office at BU. From noon to

James Ingo Freed (b. 1930)

Born on June 23, 1930, in Essen, Germany, James Freed escaped from Germany with his sister in 1939. The two children went to relatives in Chicago and their parents immigrated a year later on what he calls "one of the last boats."[11] He earned a BA in architecture in 1953 from the Illinois Institute of Technology. In 1975–1978, he returned to his alma mater as dean of the school of architecture.

The United States Holocaust Memorial Museum is located at 100 Raoul Wallenberg Place in Washington, D.C.

In 1986, the United States Holocaust Memorial Council asked James Freed to be architect for the Holocaust Memorial Museum in Washington, D.C. Night after night, as he studied, he realized how little he really knew about the Holocaust. He decided to go to Auschwitz and see the camp for himself.

> . . . there in Auschwitz on my first night in the camp it all fell apart for me . . . and I knew I had to do this for those who were gone and who [sic] we must remember and for the survivors who knew, and for those like myself who did not know but knew we did not know and who, but for the accident of time, would have known. We owed the greatest debt, for we had not only survived but had survived in ignorance.[12]

Freed claims that the strong emotion he brought back with him "remains in the work."[13] What he has designed—a memorial and a museum—is a place every American owns and can experience.

3:00 he taught a course called "Responses to Jewish Suffering" and then met with one of his Ph.D. candidates afterwards. He met with John Silber, the University president, ate a modest dinner, and then delivered a lecture about Noah at 7:00 P.M. He caught the last shuttle back to New York and reached his apartment about 11:00. He went to bed at 1:00 and rose five hours later to begin writing.[14]

A Medal and a Wreath

In 1985, United States President Ronald Reagan announced that Chancellor Helmut Kohl of West Germany had invited him to pay an official state visit. The two countries had been allies and friends since the Cold War had begun in the 1950s. Administration spokespersons explained that an official state visit would show that the past was buried and both nations had moved on.

That same year, Wiesel was to be awarded the Congressional Gold Medal for humanitarian leadership on behalf of the people of the United States. This prestigious and rare honor would take place in a White House ceremony. A gold medal with Wiesel's likeness was designed and created by the U.S. Mint. The words AUTHOR—TEACHER—WITNESS are engraved upon it. Wiesel would make a speech that many people would hear.

As the award ceremony was being planned, Reagan announced that while he visited Germany, he would place a wreath at Bitburg Cemetery. For Wiesel, this was absolutely, unequivocally wrong because Nazi soldiers, members of Hitler's SS, are buried there. For months, on television and in print, Wiesel begged the president to change his plans. Just when Wiesel was being nationally honored for his courage and compassion, he became the president's most outspoken critic. The day of his speech approached and no one was sure what Wiesel would say. Would he confront the president of the United States head-on?

Reagan's staff relocated the Gold Medal ceremony to a smaller room to ensure a smaller audience. In characteristic style, Wiesel spoke with brevity and candor. In his speech, he evoked his most horrible memories of life in the death camps: "One million children perished. If I spent my entire life reciting their names, I would die before finishing the task.

Elie Wiesel was disappointed when President Ronald Reagan (second from left in foreground) visited a graveyard where SS soldiers were buried. To the left of Reagan is his wife, Nancy, and to the right is West German chancellor Helmut Kohl and his wife, Hannelore.

Children . . . I have seen some of them thrown into the flames
. . . alive."[15] He spoke in a most public ceremony, amidst TV
cameras and reporters, crammed into a room too small to hold
them, in a speech that called upon the president to make a
choice, not a political or economic choice, but a *moral* choice:
"I . . . implore you, Mr. President, in the spirit of this moment
that justifies so many others, tell us now that you will not go
there: *that* place is not your place. Your place is with the
victims of the S.S."[16] The president was moved to tears.

Despite Wiesel's passion, President Reagan went to
Bitburg—and he placed a wreath in a cemetery that entombed
SS soldiers. The president justified his choice by claiming that
the SS soldiers were victims, too. (To the contrary, the
Nuremberg Trials declared all SS members collectively
guilty.) In Wiesel's opinion, the act was blasphemy. When
asked to comment, he told a television crew, "With these few
steps taken by the President, forty years of history have been
wiped out."[17]

And yet, the controversy received tremendous amounts
of international publicity. For weeks, all over the world,
people were discussing what President Reagan should do. The
dramatic dialogue, via its media coverage, heightened
American awareness of collective memory and public policy.
Wiesel had become a moral leader—not just of Holocaust
survivors or Jews—but of all Americans. Soon, he would be
recognized as a moral leader of all of the citizens of the world.

Honor

At about 4:00 P.M. on Yom Kippur, October 13, 1986, Elie and Marion walked home from the synagogue. They found a visitor waiting for them. He was a reporter from *Dagbladet*, a Norwegian newspaper. He handed Marion a bouquet of flowers and asked for an exclusive interview the following day. He did not give a reason.

The next morning, Elie and Marion rose at 4:00 A.M. Their good friends Sigmund, Yossi, and Per, came to their house in anticipation of what was about to happen. At 5:00 A.M. (mid-morning in Oslo), the telephone rang. Jakub Sverdrup, the director of the Nobel committee, announced that by a unanimous vote, Elie Wiesel would be awarded the 1986 Nobel Peace Prize, the world's greatest humanitarian honor. Overwhelmed by emotion, the group of friends embraced for a quiet moment. Then the phone began to ring—and it did not stop for days.

Wiesel called Hilda who was overjoyed. He agreed to attend a press conference at the Ninety-second Street YM-YWHA.

Outside the local French restaurant where Wiesel's family and friends went for a celebratory dinner, people burst into spontaneous applause when they saw him on the sidewalk. At home, near midnight, they found more reporters and journalists—and telegrams of congratulations from all over the world.

In the midst of all this media attention, Wiesel got a call from Peter Uberroth, then commissioner of Major League Baseball. He asked Wiesel to throw out the first pitch in the World Series. Not a sports fan, Wiesel barely understood what the World Series was.[1] After some negotiating because of Shabbat and its restrictions, they agreed on a later game, and Elie Wiesel pitched a baseball for the first, and probably last, time in his life. The day after the game, his photograph adorned the front page of the *New York Times* sports section.

On December 9, 1986, Marion, Elisha, and Elie Wiesel traveled to Oslo, Norway, to attend the Nobel ceremonies. They stayed in the Nobel Suite in the Grand Hotel where there were flowers and chocolates and press conferences. That afternoon, Wiesel attended a private audience with Olaf V, the King of Norway, who reminisced about his own experiences during World War II. That night, at the official ceremony, Egil Aarvik, chairperson of the Nobel committee, gave a speech that included these words:

> Today . . . the Peace Prize is to be presented to one who survived. In 1945, on the ashes left behind after the sacrificial flames which annihilated six million Jews, sat the seventeen-year-old Elie Wiesel, an only son of Abraham, an Isaac who once again had escaped a sacrificial death on Mount Moriah at the last moment. He will receive the Nobel Peace Prize today because he, too, has become a witness for truth and justice. From the abyss of the death camps he has come as a messenger to mankind—not with a message of hate and revenge, but

with one of brotherhood and atonement. He has become a powcrful spokesman for the view of mankind and the unlimited humanity which is, at all times, the basis of a lasting peace. Elie Wiesel is not only the man who survived—he is also the spirit which has conquered. In him we see a man who has climbed from utter humiliation to become one of our most important spiritual leaders and guides. . . .

I doubt whether any other individual, through the use of such quiet speech, has achieved more or been more widely heard. The words are not big, and the voice which speaks them is low. It is a voice of peace we hear. But the power is intense. . . .

It is in recognition of this particular human spirit's victory over the powers of death and degradation, and as a support to the rebellion of good against evil in the world, that the Norwegian Nobel Committee today presents the Nobel Peace Prize to Elie Wiesel. We do this on behalf of millions—from all peoples and races. We do it in deep reverence for the memory of the dead, but also with the deep felt hope that the prize will be a small contribution which will forward the cause which is the greatest of all humanity's concerns—the cause of peace.[2]

As Aarvik spoke, memories of Sighet, his father, his mother, and his little sister flooded Wiesel's mind. He could hardly contain his emotion; in fact, he could not speak.[3] Later that evening, after a torchlight parade, a formal dinner, and several other speeches, Wiesel delivered his "Nobel Address," beginning with a prayer *Ani Maamin* (" I Believe"), which he sang. It was the first time a Nobel prize winner had sung during his or her acceptance.

The days following brought a flood of communication. Today, in the archives at Boston University, huge boxes hold hundreds of cards, telegrams, and newspaper clips all dated October 1986. In all languages they came, from Jews and gentiles, from old and young, from survivors and students—a chorus of congratulations from all over the world. The good wishes took many forms, from humble handwritten notes to generous gifts. One was from Rabbi Menashe Klein, Wiesel's friend since Buna. Klein announced the creation of a house of study and prayer in Israel, a *Beit Hamidrash*, raised in honor of and named for Shlomo Wiesel.

Planted in the Future

Three months after receiving the Nobel Peace Prize, Elie Wiesel used the cash award to create the Elie Wiesel Foundation for Humanity with his wife, Marion. The foundation's aim was to serve "the cause of peace." The foundation's mission is to advance the cause of human rights by creating forums for the discussion and resolution of urgent ethical issues.

The foundation seeks to combat indifference, intolerance, and injustice through several programs. International conferences and seminars gather scholars, artists, scientists, and statesmen from all over the world. For example, "Facing the 21st Century: Threats & Promises," a meeting of more than seventy Nobel Laureates in Paris in 1988; "Saving Our Children" in New York in 1992; and "The Future of Hope in Hiroshima," in 1995. In an essay contest for college juniors and seniors, participants reflect on their most profound moral dilemmas and analyze what they have learned about ethics. A Humanitarian Award recognizes outstanding individuals whose accomplishments are consistent with the goals of the Foundation. Winners have included First Lady of France Danielle Mitterrand in 1989 for her work with children in Third World countries; U.S. President George Bush in 1991 for opposing tyranny and defending democratic ideals during the Gulf War; and His Majesty King Juan Carlos of Spain, also

in 1991 for bringing democracy to his country through peaceful means. Named for Wiesel's younger sister, the Beit Tzipora Centers support Ethiopian-Jewish children. Two after-school programs in Ashkelon and Kiryat Malachi offer academic, emotional, and social support to about one thousand boys and girls.

Today, nearly one generation after, the Elie Wiesel Foundation for Humanity remains vibrant and self-sustaining. Wiesel's work, for so long rooted in the past, and then, during his years as journalist and teacher, in the present, is now, thanks to the Nobel Prize, firmly planted in the future.

"In a Certain Tone of Voice"

A year later, in 1987, Wiesel was again transported to the past. The Nazi Klaus Barbie was brought to trial in France. Known as the "Butcher of Lyons," he was responsible for the deaths of hundreds of French Resistance members and thousands of Jews. He had deported almost eight thousand Jews to the concentration camps. After the war, he secretly served as a U.S. army agent in Germany. In 1951 he fled Europe for Bolivia. Identified by Nazi-hunters in the early 1970s, he was expelled from Bolivia in 1983, and came to trial in France in 1987.

The prosecutors asked Wiesel to testify against Barbie even though he had been nowhere near Lyons, France, during the war. Wiesel had been following the trial through the media and had heard the testimonies of many of Barbie's victims.

....

The Nobel Peace Prize was Elie Wiesel's opportunity to address the world . . . and its citizens have often listened.

The Nobel Acceptance Speech Delivered by Elie Wiesel

Oslo, Norway, December 10, 1986

Your Majesty, Your Royal Highnesses, Your Excellencies, Chairman Aarvik, members of the Nobel Committee, ladies and gentlemen:

Words of gratitude. First to our common Creator. This is what the Jewish tradition commands us to do. On special occasions, one is duty bound to recite the following prayer: *Barukh shehekhyanu vekiymanu vehigianu lazman haze*— "Blessed be Thou for having sustained us until this day."

Then—thank you, Chairman Aarvik, for the depth of your eloquence. And for the generosity of your gesture. Thank you for building bridges between people and generations. Thank you, above all, for helping humankind make peace its most urgent and noble aspiration.

I am moved, deeply moved by your words, Chairman Aarvik. And it is with a profound sense of humility that I accept the honor—the highest there is—that you have chosen to bestow upon me. I know: your choice transcends my person.

Do I have the right to represent the multitudes who have perished? Do I have the right to accept this great honor on their behalf? I do not. No one may speak for the dead, no one may interpret their mutilated dreams and visions. And yet, I sense their presence. I always do—and at this moment more than ever. The presence of my parents, that of my little sister. The presence of my teachers, my friends, my companions. . . .

This honor belongs to all the survivors and their children and, through us, to the Jewish people with whose destiny I have always identified.

I remember: it happened yesterday or eternities ago. A young Jewish boy discovered the Kingdom of Night. I remember his bewilderment, I remember his anguish. It all happened so fast.

The ghetto. The deportation. The sealed cattle car. The fiery altar upon which the history of our people and the future of mankind were meant to be sacrificed.

I remember he asked his father, "Can this be true? This is the twentieth century, not the Middle Ages. Who would allow such crimes to be committed? How could the world remain silent?"

And now the boy is turning to me. "Tell me," he asks, "what have you done with my future? What have you done with your life?" And I tell him that I have tried. That I have tried to keep memory alive, that I have tried to fight those who would forget. Because if we forget, we are guilty, we are accomplices.

And then I explain to him how naïve we were—that the world did know and remained silent. And that is why I swore never to be silent whenever and wherever human beings endure suffering and humiliation. We must take sides. Neutrality helps the oppressor, never the victim. Silence encourages the tormentor, never the tormented. Sometimes we must interfere. When human lives are endangered, when human dignity is in jeopardy, national borders and sensitivities become irrelevant. Wherever men or women are persecuted because of their race, religion, or political views, that place must—at that moment—become the center of the universe.

Of course, since I am a Jew profoundly rooted in my people's memory and tradition, my first response is to Jewish fears, Jewish needs, Jewish crises. For I belong to a traumatized generation, one that experienced the abandonment and solitude of our people. It would be unnatural for me not to make Jewish priorities my own: Israel, Soviet Jewry, Jews in Arab land. . . . But others are important to me. Apartheid is, in my view, as abhorrent as anti-Semitism. To me, Andrei Sakharov's isolation is as much a disgrace as Joseph Begun's imprisonment and Ida Nudel's exile. As is the denial of

Solidarity and its leader Lech Walesa's right to dissent. And Nelson Mandela's interminable imprisonment.

There is so much injustice and suffering crying out for our attention: victims of hunger, of racism and political persecution—in Chile, for instance, or in Ethiopia—writers and poets, prisoners in so many lands governed by the Left and by the Right.

Human rights are being violated on every continent. More people are oppressed than free. How can one not be sensitive to their plight? Human suffering anywhere concerns men and women everywhere. That applies also to the Palestinians, to whose plight I am sensitive, but whose methods I deplore when they lead to violence. Violence is not the answer. Terrorism is the most dangerous of answers. They are frustrated, that is understandable; something must be done. The refugees and their misery; the children and their fears; the uprooted and their hopelessness: something must be done about their situation. Both the Jewish people and the Palestinian people have lost too many sons and daughters and have shed too much blood. This must stop, and all attempts to stop it must be encouraged. Israel will cooperate, I am sure of that. I trust Israel, for I have faith in the Jewish people. Let Israel be given a chance, let hatred and danger be removed from her horizons, and there will be peace in and around the Holy Land. Please understand my deep and total commitment to Israel: if you could remember what I remember, you *would* understand. Israel is the only nation in the world whose very existence is threatened. Should Israel lose but one war, it would mean her end and ours as well. But I have faith. Faith in the God of Abraham, Isaac, and Jacob, and even in His creation. Without it no action would be possible. And action is the only remedy to indifference, the most insidious danger of all. Isn't that the meaning of Alfred Nobel's legacy? Wasn't his fear of war a shield against war?

There is so much to be done, there is so much that can be done. One person—a Raoul Wallenberg, an Albert Schweitzer, a Martin Luther King, Jr.—one person of integrity can make a difference, a difference of life and death.

As long as one dissident is in prison, our freedom will not be true. As long as one child is hungry, our lives will be filled with anguish and shame. What all these victims need above all is to know that they are not alone; that we are not forgetting them, that when their voices are stifled we shall lend them ours, that while their freedom depends on ours, the quality of our freedom depends on theirs.

This is what I say to the young Jewish boy wondering what I have done with his years. It is in his name that I speak to you and that I express to you my deepest gratitude . . . as one who has emerged from the Kingdom of Night. We know that every moment is a moment of grace, every hour an offering; not to share them would mean to betray them.

Our lives no longer belong to us alone; they belong to all those who need us desperately.

Thank you, Chairman Aarvik. Thank you, members of the Nobel Committee. Thank you, people of Norway, for declaring on this singular occasion that our survival has meaning for mankind.[4]

For the first time, Wiesel testified in a court of law. He recognized, "This trial is necessary for the world to be able to hear certain words said in a certain tone of voice."[5] In an eloquent speech, he recalled that one SS soldier told a young Jew that even if he did survive, no one would believe his story. In fact, Wiesel said, the public trials of Nazi crimes validate the survival of the witnesses such as himself: "Their testimony counts, their memories will be part of a collective memory. Of course, nothing can bring the dead back to life. But because of the meetings that have taken place within these precincts, because of the words spoken, the accused will not be able to kill the dead again."[6] Thanks to the witnesses who testified to his crimes, Barbie was found guilty of crimes against humanity and sentenced to life imprisonment. He died in prison in 1991.

During this time—as he always has—Wiesel continued to write. In 1988, he published *The Six Days of Destruction*, written with Rabbi Albert Friedlander. In it, the authors weave personal stories of six Holocaust victims with the narratives of the six biblical days of creation. *Six Days* is his literary attempt to reconcile past with present and see the events of his own lifetime mirrored in Jewish history. Also in 1998, Wiesel returned to the novel as literary form, continuing his tradition of weaving biography with imagination. *Twilight* portrays a literature professor who searches for a mysterious mentor in a mental asylum.

Consumed With Reminding

With a lower case *h*, the word *holocaust* means a ritual offering that is completely consumed by fire. Many historians give Elie Wiesel credit for first using the word in a new way. With a capital *H*, Holocaust refers to the systematic, genocidal destruction of 6 million Jews by the Nazis before and during

World War II. Most of their bodies were consumed by fire. For the last fifty years, Elie Wiesel has been consumed with reminding the world to remember and not to repeat. Much of his humanitarian efforts, and so much of his travel, is dedicated to this work, such as his trips to Cambodia in 1980, to Nicaragua in 1982, and to South Africa in 1985.

In 1992, it seemed that history may have been repeating itself in the area of Europe that was formerly Yugoslavia. After the fall of communism, many small republics declared their independence. In Serbia, one of the new republics, the Serbs were trying to forcibly remove any person who was not a "true Serb." Slobodan Milosevic's racist policy of "ethnic cleansing" echoed that of the Nazis. Wiesel made a trip to Bosnia in November 1992 to express his outrage and to call public attention to the situation by drawing parallels to the Holocaust. "He was 'eloquent', reported *The Times*, 'in his denunciation of the detention camps; so much so that Radovan Karadzic, the Bosnian Serb leader, promised to empty Serb-controlled camps immediately.'"[7]

Fruition

On April 19, 1993, on the fiftieth anniversary of the Warsaw Ghetto uprising, the United States Holocaust Memorial Museum opened, ten years after its was commissioned by the U.S. government. As a living testimony, a bearer of witness, a research institute, an educational program, and an archive, the USHMM is unprecedented. President Bill Clinton officiated and Elie Wiesel delivered an improvised speech in which he evoked a memory of his mother, in her kitchen, preparing for Passover in 1943. Even on this public occasion, Wiesel continued to fight against silence. In the midst of his speech, he turned to President Clinton and urged him to do something to stop the bloodshed in Sarajevo. Later, he was criticized for using the opening ceremony to launch a personal, political appeal. His answer to his critics was firm: ". . . when men are dying, when innocent people are subjected to rape and torture, when cities are being transformed into cemeteries, Jews do not have the right to be silent."[8]

Today, the United States Holocaust Memorial Museum houses both permanent and temporary exhibition spaces, a research library and archives, two theaters, a computer learning center, classrooms, 26,000 authentic Holocaust artifacts, and the haunting, hexagonal Hall of Remembrance. It is a narrative museum, which means that, as visitors pass through it, they experience a story from beginning to middle to end. This living memorial stirs the emotions. It conjures horror, sadness, and hope. It disturbs. As of March 1, 2004, more than 20 million visitors have experienced its tunnels, stairs, walls, ramps, and windows. This includes 6.3 million children and 2.4 million international visitors. It also includes 14.9 million non-Jews and 76 heads of state.[9]

Wiesel saved his opinion of the museum for the second volume of his memoirs, published in 1999. He admires the power of the building and praises the tremendous collective effort. And yet, for him, something essential is simply not there. "I would have preferred a more sober, more humble edifice, one that would suggest the unspoken, the silence, the secret . . . Here, the sense of mystery is missing."[10]

Amidst so much public acclaim, more books in more forms came to fruition during the 1990s. In another novel, *The Forgotten* (1992), a Holocaust survivor loses his memory to Alzheimer's disease. In 1993, Wiesel wrote personal remembrances to accompany *A Passover Haggadah*, the prayers that Jews recite each spring. *King Solomon and His Magic Ring* (1999) is an illustrated children's book based on a Biblical tale.

François Mitterrand (1916–1996)

It was often said that young François Mitterrand would not be part of any group unless he could be its leader. He attended college in Paris where he studied law and political science, but he joined the infantry when World War II broke out in France.

In 1940, when France fell to the Nazis, Mitterrand was badly wounded and imprisoned in a German camp. On his third attempt, he escaped from camp and made his way back to France. At first, he worked for Marshall Petain's Vichy pro-Nazi government, but he soon joined the French Resistance movement. After the war, he became one of the youngest members of the new French government. Over the next twenty years, Mitterrand held several cabinet posts, including secretary of state and minister of justice.

During those decades, Mitterrand had swung from the far right to the far left and became a socialist. During his third bid for the presidency in 1981, no one thought he would win. His victory surprised the world.

Mitterrand served as France's president for fourteen years. His vision of a more united Europe guided his policy. He is remembered by historians as a highly skilled politician, who was able to divide his enemies and use his power decisively. He abolished the death penalty and restored the Louvre Museum. Like Wiesel, Mitterrand was an eloquent speaker and writer. He died of pancreatic cancer in 1996.

His two-volume memoir, *All Rivers Run to the Sea* (1995) and *And the Sea Is Never Full* (1999) offer personal reflections on Wiesel's own rich life. The memoirs total over eight hundred pages.

In addition to books written by Wiesel, many people have published books about him. Several are based on interviews. Even in print, Wiesel's quiet, gentle voice contrasts with the loud, fast flood of words that overwhelm our modern ears. In *A Journey of Faith* (1990), Wiesel converses with Catholic Cardinal John O'Connor. *Evil and Exile* (1990) contains interviews with French journalist Michael de Saint-Cheron; *Memoir in Two Voices* (1996) with the former President of France, François Mitterrand; and *Conversations with Elie Wiesel* (2001) with historian Richard Heffner. However, one of these collaborations was a source of despair. Despite its publication, Wiesel denounces one of these books entirely.

Mitterrand's Alliances

Soon after François Mitterrand became president of France in 1985, he and Elie Wiesel became close intellectual friends. They met often, and discussed politics, art, religion, and philosophy, despite obvious differences. One was Catholic; the other Jewish. One was a politician; the other a writer. They disagreed about many things, most dramatically about Palestinian leader Yasser Arafat's visit to Paris. For Wiesel, Arafat represented the greatest political threat to the annihilation of Israel: that is, the Palestinian claim to the same piece of land. When Arafat visited Mitterrand, Wiesel saw it as a conciliatory gesture toward an enemy of Israel. Despite their differences, the two learned men respected each other. In fact, they agreed to publish a series of "dialogues" based on their conversations as *A Memoir in Two Voices*.

Their friendship grew and deepened through an entire decade. In September 1994, a book was published that described Mitterrand's alliances with Nazi sympathizers, even with Nazi supporters, early in the history of occupied France. He later became part of the French Resistance movement, but the book confirmed that there were Nazi skeletons in Mitterrand's closet. Wiesel wanted his friend to publicly acknowledge his past and apologize, thereby setting an example for others like him, but Mitterrand refused to express regret or remorse. Instead, he claimed ignorance, a defense Wiesel neither believed nor accepted. This was a disagreement Wiesel refused to move past, for it went to the very heart of his life's work—bearing witness and exposing the truth, no matter how painful either may be.

Wiesel is not proud of *A Memoir in Two Voices*. He has written that he no longer considers the book his.[11] Soon after the book was published, Mitterrand delivered a speech in which he praised Germany and honored its history without making any mention of the Third Reich. Mitterrand died in 1996, the same year the book was published, having never made a public peace with his past. Today, Wiesel mourns the loss of their friendship.

Two Generations After

In February 1995, Wiesel returned to Poland as President Clinton's representative to the fiftieth anniversary of the liberation of Auschwitz.

The planning of the commemorative event brought to light one of Wiesel's deepest fears. As the organizers prepared for the ceremony at which many leaders and dignitaries would be present, Wiesel accused them of trying to "de-Judaize" the tragedy. He believed that the people who were staging the event were avoiding the idea of Jewishness. For example,

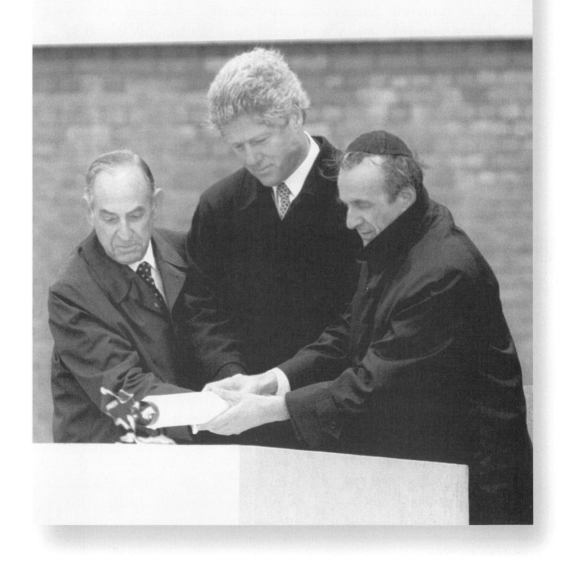

they planned to recite the Jewish prayer for the dead—Kaddish —*after* the official event. Also, despite the fact that 90 percent of the 2 million victims of Auschwitz were Jewish, the language of the ceremony did not include the words "Jewish" or "Jew."

In 1995, Lech Walesa was president of the Polish Republic. Elie Wiesel had worked with him in 1988 when they both traveled to Auschwitz and Birkenau with the President's Commission on the Holocaust. On the evening before the anniversary ceremony, Wiesel was granted a private audience with Walesa. In this meeting, Wiesel made his fears and wishes clear. He wanted Kaddish recited at the *beginning* of the official ceremony. He also wanted everyone to be reminded, again and again, that the Holocaust is, above all, a Jewish tragedy. Walesa listened, agreed, and kept his word. In his speech, the president of Poland spoke of the uniqueness of the Jewish experience. And Kaddish? It was moved to the first place in the ceremony—for everyone to hear.

Awards and Degrees

Wiesel's list of literary and humanitarian awards dates from 1963, and numbers over 120. Among them are the Prix Rivarol (1963), the National Jewish Book Council Literary Award (1965), the first Jewish Heritage Award of B'nai B'rith (1966), the first Annual Anne Frank Award (1985), and the Medal of Jerusalem (1986). In 1968, he received the Prix Medicis, one of France's most distinguished literary awards.

From left to right, United States Holocaust Memorial council chairman Harvey Meyerhoff, President Clinton, and Elie Wiesel light the eternal flame at the opening ceremony of the United States Holocaust Memorial Museum in Washington, D.C., on April 19, 1993.

For his humanitarian work he earned the U.S. Congressional Gold Medal in 1985, the Medal of Liberty in 1986, and the Presidential Medal of Freedom in 1992. Today, he serves on seven editorial advisory boards and over sixty boards of directors and committees including universities, public service organizations, Jewish foundations, and human rights councils. Often in the last forty years, he has served as leader of these efforts.

In addition, Wiesel has received no less than 125 honorary doctoral degrees from institutions of higher learning, beginning with the Jewish Theological Seminary in 1967 and including Boston University, Wesleyan, Georgetown, Tufts, Emory, Brandeis, LaSalle, Clark, American, and Loyola Universities; France's Sorbonne; and scores of colleges throughout the world.[12] In addition to teaching and lecturing, traveling and meeting, Elie Wiesel organizes, attends, and leads dozens of conferences every year.

10

Gadol b'Israel
(A Great Man of Israel)

Winning the Nobel Peace Prize gave Elie Wiesel a platform from which to speak to the entire world. Today, well into his seventies, Elie Wiesel continues the work for which the prize recognized him: teaching, writing, traveling, organizing, lecturing, and leading. For example, his interview for National Public Radio helped celebrate the one-hundredth anniversary of the Nobel Peace Prize in April 2001. He has lead conferences such as the Conference on Global Anti-Semitism in October 2002. Elie and Marion Wiesel sponsor a series of symposia around the world called "Anatomy of Hate" that brings together leaders of opposing groups such as Israelis and Palestinians; Catholics and Protestants in Northern Ireland; Serbs, Bosnians, and Croats in the Balkans. In 2002, in an eloquent documentary, *Elie Wiesel Goes Home*, cameras followed him to Sighet, and during that year, he opened a museum in his hometown. He has delivered lectures such as *An Evening with Elie Wiesel* at universities coast to coast and others as varied as "Tomorrow's Leaders" for high school sophomores and "Hope, Healing, Reconciliation, and the Renewal of the Human Spirit" to adults. On September 30, 2003, he celebrated his seventy-fifth birthday at the Waldorf-Astoria Hotel in New York City with seven hundred guests. The evening raised over $1.5 million for the Anti-Defamation League and the Elie Wiesel Foundation for Humanity. In 2004, he was interviewed by his longtime friend Ted Koppel for the closing episode of *UpClose*. He continues to answer hundreds of letters from young people who have read his books, and continues to teach in the Boston University department of Theology and lecture in both New York City and Boston. In April 2004, Wiesel delivered the opening lecture at the Organization for Security and Cooperation in Europe (OSCE) in Berlin, Germany. Held in a building that once housed Nazi Germany's central bank, and attended by representatives from fifty-five nations, the conference addressed the resurgence of anti-Semitism in Europe. At this writing, his weekly schedules continue to span both the continent and the globe.

More than forty years after publishing *Night*, Wiesel is still writing. In 2002, he published *The Judges*, a well-received novel in which five airline passengers going to Israel are caught in a snowstorm and forced to land in upstate New York. They take refuge in a house owned by a mysterious man. Each passenger has a secret and the Judge reveals, in the midst of the raging snowstorm, that one of them will be sacrificed before the night is over. Writes one reviewer,

> Wiesel concludes his novel in a manner that invites the reader to further ponder basic theological issues such as the relationship of God to historical events, the question of faith and doubt, and the continuing fascination with evil . . . The question of God in all of this, a fundamental query in Wiesel's work, is wisely left open.[1]

The Judges was followed the same year by two collections of essays and interviews. Another novel published only in French and another collection of Biblical, Talmudic, and Hasidic portraits followed in 2003. There is every indication that the canon will continue to grow as long as Wiesel can hold a pen.

What Others Say About Him

A 1999 article in *Biography Magazine* describes Wiesel's eyes as "large and dark—and very, very sad."[2] Wiesel acknowledges this reputation for sadness but also acknowledges his ability to make others laugh. "My lectures are full of laughs. People laugh and laugh and laugh. I like humor."[3] Whether they focus on Wiesel's smile or his sad eyes, he has been the subject of many observations.

Since 1974, in addition to the canon above, over fifty books have been written and published *about* Elie Wiesel, including biographies for young people, literary analyses, responses, interpretations, celebrations, tributes—and even CliffsNotes. In addition to his own words, there is no lack of words written—and spoken—about him.

> He has the look of Lazarus about him.
> > —*François Mauriac [Lazarus is a man in the Bible who is said to have risen from the dead.]*[4]

> . . . through his books, he has erected a monument to the dead, not of dead stone nor cold marble but of living works of vital importance . . . For the survivors, he has been a leader and teacher, a beacon in the darkness of our isolation. He has taught us that revenge is not our way to go; that it is the duty of every human being to reduce sufferings, not to enhance them.
> > —*Leo Eitenger, the Norwegian doctor who helped operate on Elie Wiesel in Auschwitz*[5]

Selected Works* by Elie Wiesel

Dawn, novel (1961)

The Accident, novel (1962)

The Town Beyond the Wall, novel (1964)

The Gates of the Forest, novel (1966)

A Beggar in Jerusalem, novel (1970)

The Oath, novel (1973)

A Jew Today, essays, stories, and dialogues (1978)

The Testament, novel (1981)

The Golem, legend (1983)

The Fifth Son, novel (1985)

A Song for Hope, cantata (1987)

Twilight, novel (1988)

The Forgotten, novel (1992)

King Solomon and His Magic Ring, children's book (1999)

The Judges, novel (2002)

Le temps des déracinés, novel (2003)

* Note: Elie Wiesel's nonfiction works are featured in the "Further Reading" section starting on p. 154.

He is the closest thing we have in the Jewish community to a superstar. He is the only person who, by his name alone, can produce a crowd of people and an aura of anticipation. People come to him already emotionally charged. He is a tremendous energizer to American Jewry.

> —*Rabbi Eugene Borowitz, editor of the journal Sh-ma* [6]

Wiesel possesses what might be called reverse charisma; he transfixes audiences not with bombast but with a soft, weary voice, punctuated by silences. It forces a listener to perch on the edge of the seat, neck extended, ear turned to the lectern to catch every utterance.

> —*Samuel J. Freedman in the New York Times, 1983* [7]

In assessing the life of this great and humble man, what is often unappreciated is what Elie Wiesel did not do . . . Consider what others, who have experienced lesser tragedies, have done in response to such evil. They have sought revenge. They have continued the cycles of violence and recrimination. They have become terrorists. They have refused to make peace. They have become cynics. Elie Wiesel rejected the negative path. He showed the way from brutal victimization to gentle kindness. His very life became a shining example of an alternative to the cycle of violence and retaliation which has characterized history for millennia.

> —*Alan Dershowitz, author and Harvard University professor of Law* [8]

It happens frequently in Wiesel's writing: a story is told, a line of argument is developed, and there is only one possible conclusion . . . And then, two words intrude, usually repeated: "And yet, and yet . . . " *Et pourtant, et pourtant . . .* They are less a formula than a signal. They may be Wiesel's two most important words. For they signal that conclusions do not have to follow from premises, that directions can be reversed, that there are new possibilities beyond what we anticipated, that we are not locked into ineluctable patterns.

> —Robert McAfee Brown, theologian, literary critic, and
> member of the U.S. Holocaust Memorial Council [9]

So how are we to react to the reflections of Wiesel and other Holocaust authors' autobiographies? We must offer them gratitude. Each could have easily and understandably concluded that "I have been through enough; I want to forget." Instead, each, like Wiesel, has felt a debt to both the past and the future. Wiesel has written that for him, each word he writes is a tombstone, dedicated to memorializing a death.

> —Harry James Cargas, university professor,
> Catholic member of the Executive Committee
> of the U.S. Holocaust Memorial Council [10]

Elie, the world needs you to carry on doing what you do best. And that is to speak out, build bridges, and raise the alarm about the wrongs afflicting our world. . . . The world knows you for your permanently furrowed brow, and for a face that communicates so well the anguish of the human condition. I hope that tonight, at least, you will smile as friends and admirers from around the world sing your praises.

> —Kofi Annan, Secretary-General of the
> United Nations, upon the occasion of
> Elie Wiesel's seventy-fifth birthday [11]

Coming Full Circle

The windows of Wiesel's study open out to Central Park, but Wiesel sits with his back to the view. He faces a wall as he works. At eye level in front of him hangs a black-and-white photograph of the stone house on Serpent Street in Sighet.

It is a constant reminder of his childhood and his roots. As far as he knows, his watch is still buried there.

In fact, this home and his family are still with him every day as he reads and writes, travels and eats, questions and dreams. Their presence is both comfort and burden:

> My father taught me how to reason, how to reach my mind. My soul belonged to my grandfather and my mother. They influenced me profoundly, to this day. When I write, I have the feeling, literally, physically, that one of them is behind my back, looking over my shoulder and reading what I'm writing. I'm terribly afraid of their judgment.[12]

Wiesel concludes the second volume of his memoirs by evoking the names of his childhood family. Now well into his seventies, he still teaches, writes, and travels all over the world. His sister Hilda lives in Nice, France. He may see another kind of night on his horizon, but this one offers mystery rather than horror.

> Twilight is approaching, and I know that soon it will clasp me into its mysterious folds. You [Shlomo] will be there, and you will lead me to the others . . . Grandfather Dodye and Grandmother Nissel. And mother. And Tzipora. And Bea. And all the uncles, the aunts, the cousins, the friends. I know that when I shall join your ranks, I will hear your voice at last.[13]

As he contemplates his life coming full circle, Wiesel takes pride in his son. Elisha is now a man with a life of his own, but his father remains intensely protective of his son's privacy. "[My son Elisha] is the center of my life. The center of my center . . . I am a crazy father. But he doesn't like me to speak about him."[14]

Building Bridges

United Nations Secretary-General Kofi Annan called Elie Wiesel a bridge builder. He builds bridges between individuals at meetings and symposia, between presidents in conference rooms, and between students and teachers everywhere. In addition, the Elie Wiesel Foundation for Humanity sponsors an annual essay contest that welcomes writing by college students on any topic related to the domain of ethics. In 2004, for the first time, the essays were available to the public, and the bridge for ideas is as broad as the World Wide Web. Recent winning essays include "Forty-three Cents," a personal reflection on Tibetan children; "Chasing Images of the Dead: The Unreality of the Iraq War in American Media"; and "The Burden of Lightness," a literary analysis exploring the immobility that can evolve from spiritual heaviness.

In July 2001, the United States House of Representatives established the Elie Wiesel Youth Leadership Congressional Fellowship Program in which high school students—one from each congressional district—participate in leadership and ethics courses offered by the foundation in Washington, D.C. Young people experience firsthand their nation's capital, discuss the complexities of ethical choices, and learn to build bridges of their own.

This photograph of Elie and Marion appeared in a 1982 *People* magazine article. Wiesel's two-volume memoir is titled *All Rivers Run to the Sea: Memoirs* (1995) and *And the Sea Is Never Full: Memoirs 1969–* (1999).

What Can I Do?

For Elic Wicscl, what cach individual can do is simplc. We can read. We can learn. We can act. We can teach others. We can remember. We can reject intolerance in any form, and by doing so, we can honor those millions of victims whom Wiesel has carried in his heart every day of his long life. Most importantly, we can fight indifference, for it is the real enemy of all citizens of a moral world. As you read the words below, imagine a live and gentle voice speaking with an accent still seasoned with Yiddish, Romanian, and French. As you read, imagine that the voice is speaking directly to you.

> I have always felt that the opposite of culture is not ignorance; it's indifference. And the opposite of faith is not atheism; again, it's indifference. And the opposite of morality is not immorality; it's again indifference.[15]

> Indifference is not a beginning, it is an end. And, therefore, indifference is always the friend of the enemy, for it benefits the aggressor—never his victim, whose pain is magnified when he or she feels forgotten. The political prisoner in his cell, the hungry children, the homeless refugees—not to respond to their plight, not to relieve their solitude by offering them a spark of hope is to exile them from human memory. And in denying their humanity we betray our own.[16]

Dayyenu

There is a Hebrew word that Elie Wiesel likes to slip into his writing. The word is *dayyenu* and it means "it would have been enough."

If Elie Wiesel had only written *Night*, *dayyenu*. If he had written fifty other books but not become an journalist, *dayyenu*. If he were a journalist but never married, *dayyenu*. If he were a husband and father but not a respected professor, *dayyenu*. If he were a beloved university professor but not the "conscience of the Holocaust," *dayyenu*. If he were "the conscience of the Holocaust" but had not inspired a museum, *dayyenu*. If he inspired a museum but had not won the Nobel Peace Prize, *dayyenu*. If he won the Nobel Peace Prize but had not influenced presidents, *dayyenu*. If he influenced presidents but had not become a moral leader of the free world, *dayyenu*.

But, in fact, Elie Wiesel has done all of this. He experienced the worst side of human nature and emerged a *gadol b'Israel*—a great man of Israel—fulfilling the rabbi's prophecy and his father's prayers.

TIMELINE

(Shaded areas indicate events in the life of Elie Wiesel.)

1922

Hilda Wiesel born, daughter of Sarah Feig and Shlomo Wiesel, in Sighet, Romania.

1926

Bea Wiesel born.

1928

September 30: Elie Wiesel born.

1929

October: New York stock market crash.

1931

Elie enrolls in school and begins to learn Hebrew.

1933

Hitler becomes chancellor of Germany.

March 22: Concentration camp at Dachau opens.

April 26: Gestapo established.

May 10: Nazis burn banned books in public.

1934

August 2: Hitler names himself "Führer," or leader, of Germany.

1935

Tzipora Wiesel born.

May 31: Jews in Germany no longer allowed to serve in armed forces.

September 15: Anti-Jewish Nuremberg Laws are enacted; Jews are no longer considered citizens of Germany.

1936

Nazis boycott Jewish-owned businesses.

March 7: Nazis occupy Rhineland.

July: Sachsenhausen concentration camp opens.

1937

July 15: Buchenwald concentration camp opens.

138

1938

March: Mauthausen concentration camp opens.

March 13: Germany annexes Austria and applies all anti-Jewish laws there.

July 6: League of Nations holds conference on Jewish refugees at Evian, France, but no action is taken to help the refugees.

October 5: All Jewish passports must now be stamped with a red "J."

October 15: Nazi troops occupy the Sudentenland.

November 9-10: Kristallnacht, the Night of the Broken Glass; Jewish businesses and synagogues are destroyed and 30,000 Jews are sent to concentration camps.

1939

March 15: Germans occupy Czechoslovakia.

August 23: Germany and the Soviet Union sign a non-aggression pact.

September 1: Germany invades Poland, beginning World War II.

October 28: First Polish ghetto established in Piotrkow, Poland.

November 23: Jews in Poland are forced to wear an arm band or yellow star.

1940

April 9: Germans occupy Denmark and southern Norway.

May 7: Lodz Ghetto is established.

May 10: Germans invade Belgium and the Netherlands.

May 20: Auschwitz concentration camp is established.

June 22: France surrenders to Germany.

September 27: Germany, Italy, and Japan form the Axis powers.

November 16: Warsaw Ghetto is established.

1941

Elie's bar mitzvah.

1941 *(continued)*

June 22: Germany invades the Soviet Union.

October: Auschwitz II (Birkenau) death camp is established.

1942

British air raids hit Amsterdam.

January 20: Wannsee Conference takes place in Berlin where the "Final Solution" is outlined.

March 17: Killings begin at Belzec death camp.

May: Killings begin at Sobibor death camp.

July 22: Treblinka concentration camp is established.

Summer–Winter: Mass deportations to death camps begin.

1943

March: Liquidation of Krakow Ghetto begins.

April 19: Warsaw ghetto uprising.

Fall: Liquidation of Minsk, Vilna, and Riga ghettos.

1944

May 16: Family deported to Auschwitz.

March-May: Germany occupies Hungary and begins deporting Hungarian Jews.

July 14: Soviet forces liberate Majdanek death camp.

November 8: Death march of Jews from Budapest to Austria begins.

1945

January 17: Auschwitz inmates begin death march.

January 29: Shlomo dies in Buchenwald.

April: Liberated from Buchenwald; Taken to France.

April 30: Hitler commits suicide.

May 8: Germany surrenders.

1946

Enrolls at Sorbonne; Moves to a Paris rooming house.

1948

Begins work as journalist for *Yedioth Ahronoth*.

1949

First trip to Israel.

1954

Writes *Un die Velt Hot Geshvign*.

1956

Hit by a car in New York City.

1958

La Nuit published in France.

1960

Night published in the United States.

1963

Receives U.S. citizenship.

1964

First return to Sighet.

1965

First trip to Soviet Union.

1969

April 2: Marries Marion Rose Erster in Jerusalem.

1972

June 6: Son Elisha is born.

1974

Sister Bea dies in Montreal.

1976

Begins lecture series at Ninety-second Street YM-YWHA in Manhattan; Named Andrew W. Mellon Professor of the Humanities at Boston University.

1978

Appointed chairperson of Presidential Commission on the Holocaust.

1980

Appointed Chairperson of U.S. Holocaust Memorial Council; Trip to Cambodia.

1981

Chairs First World Gathering of Jewish Holocaust Survivors in Jerusalem.

1985

Awarded Congressional Medal of Achievement by President Reagan.

1986

December 10: Awarded Nobel Peace Prize.

1987

Establishes Elie and Marion Wiesel Foundation for Humanity.

1992

Receives Medal of Freedom from President Bush.

1993

Visits Bosnia to "bear witness"; Principal speaker at dedication of the United States Holocaust Memorial Museum, Washington, D.C.

1995

Publishes volume I of memoirs, *All Rivers Run to the Sea.*

1999

Publishes volume II of memoirs, *And the Sea Is Never Full.*

2001

Elie Wiesel Youth Leadership Congressional Fellowship Program established.

2002

Documentary *Elie Wiesel Goes Home.*

2003

September 30: Seventy-fifth birthday celebration in New York City.

Chapter Notes

Chapter 1. The Return

1. Elie Wiesel, *All Rivers Run to the Sea: Memoirs* (New York: Alfred A. Knopf, 1995), p. 22. From ALL RIVERS RUN TO THE SEA by Elie Wiesel, copyright © 1995 by Elie Wiesel. Used by permission of Alfred A. Knopf, a division of Random House, Inc.

2. Elie Wiesel, *Legends of Our Time* (New York: Holt, Rinehart and Winston, 1968), p. 113.

3. Elie Wiesel, *One Generation After* (New York: Random House, 1965), pp. 63–64; Elie Wiesel, *From the Kingdom of Memory* (New York: Schocken Books, 1990), pp. 123–129; Wiesel, *Legends of Our Time*, pp. 110–130.

4. *First Person Singular: Elie Wiesel*, PBS DVD, Lives and Legacies Films, 2002.

5. The story told in this chapter is one that Wiesel tells again and again, in "The Last Return" in *Legends of Our Time*, in "The Watch" in *One Generation After*, in "Sighet Again" in *From the Kingdom of Memory*, in "A House of Strangers" in *A Jew Today*, on pages 358–360 of *All Rivers Run to the Sea*, in the PBS documentary *First Person Singular: Elie Wiesel*, and fictionally, in *The Town Beyond the Wall*.

Chapter 2. Sighet

1. Elie Wiesel, *Night* (New York: Avon Books, 1969), p. 13. Excerpts from NIGHT by Elie Wiesel, translated by Stella Rodway. Copyright © 1960 by MacGibbon & Kee. Copyright renewed © 1988 by The Collins Publishing Group. Reprinted by permission of Hill and Wang, a division of Farrar, Straus and Giroux, LLC.

2. Elie Wiesel, *All Rivers Run to the Sea: Memoirs* (New York: Alfred A. Knopf, 1995), p. 22. From ALL RIVERS RUN TO THE SEA by Elie Wiesel, copyright © 1995 by Elie Wiesel. Used by permission of Alfred A. Knopf, a division of Random House, Inc.

3. Raul Hilberg, *The Destruction of the European Jews*, Student Edition (New York: Holmes & Meier Publishers, Inc., 1985), pp. 66–72.

4. Ibid., p. 189.

5. Ibid., pp. 5–8.

6. Martin Gilbert, *Never Again: A History of the Holocaust* (New York: Universe Publishing, 2000), p. 21.

7. Wiesel, *All Rivers Run to the Sea*, p. 23.

8. Eric Levin, "Holocaust Survivor Elie Wiesel Decries a Rising Tide of Anti-Semitism at Home and Abroad," *People*, Vol. 9, November 29, 1982, pp. 73ff.

9. Wiesel, *All Rivers Run to the Sea*, p. 14.

10. Ibid., p. 13.

11. Ibid., p. 9.

12. Ibid., p. 10.

13. Samuel G. Freedman, "Bearing Witness: The Life and Work of Elie Wiesel," *The New York Times Magazine*, October 23, 1983, p. 65.

14. Wiesel, *All Rivers Run to the Sea*, p. 15.

15. Brigitte-Fanny Cohen, "Talking with Elie Wiesel, in *Elie Wiesel: Conversations,* ed. Robert Franciosi (Jackson: University Press of Mississippi, 2002), p. 135.

16. Wiesel, *All Rivers Run to the Sea*, p. 4.

17. Ibid., pp. 4 and 13.

18. Ibid., p. 24.

19. Ibid., p. 10.

20. Ibid., p. 25.

21. Ibid., p. 13.

Chapter 3. Yellow Stars

1. Martin Gilbert, *A History of the Twentieth Century, Volume I: 1900–1933* (New York: William Morrow & Company, Inc., 1997), p. 772.

2. Roselle Chartock and Jack Spencer, eds. *The Holocaust Years: Society on Trial* (New York: Bantam Books, 1978), p. 108.

3. Margot Stern Strom and William S. Parsons, *Facing History and Ourselves: Holocaust and Human Behavior* (Watertown, Mass.: Intentional Educations, Inc., 1982), pp. 81–82.

4. Gilbert, *History*, p. 793.

5. Adolf Hitler, *Mein Kampf*, "Chapter II—Years of Study and Suffering in Vienna," from *Nalanda Digital Library*, n.d., <http://www.nalanda.nitc.ac.in/resources/english/etext-project/Biography/hitler/volume-1chapter2.html> (December 2, 2004).

6. Raul Hilberg, *The Destruction of the European Jews*, Student Edition (New York: Holmes & Meier Publishers, Inc., 1985), p. 8.

7. Elie Wiesel, *All Rivers Run to the Sea: Memoirs* (New York: Schocken Books, Inc., 1995), p. 33. From ALL RIVERS RUN TO

THE SEA by Elie Wiesel, copyright © 1995 by Elie Wiesel. Used by permission of Alfred A. Knopf, a division of Random House, Inc.

    8. Ibid., p. 34.

    9. Ibid., p. 33.

    10. Ibid., p. 18.

    11. Martin Gilbert, *Never Again: A History of the Holocaust* (New York: Universe Publishing, 2000), pp. 70–71.

    12. Elie Wiesel, *Night* (New York: Avon Books, 1969), p. 21. Excerpts from NIGHT by Elie Wiesel, translated by Stella Rodway. Copyright © 1960 by MacGibbon & Kee. Copyright renewed © 1988 by The Collins Publishing Group. Reprinted by permission of Hill and Wang, a division of Farrar, Straus and Giroux, LLC.

Chapter 4. Death Trains

    1. Elie Wiesel, *All Rivers Run to the Sea: Memoirs* (New York: Schocken Books, Inc., 1995), p. 69. From ALL RIVERS RUN TO THE SEA by Elie Wiesel, copyright © 1995 by Elie Wiesel. Used by permission of Alfred A. Knopf, a division of Random House, Inc.

    2. Ibid., p. 75.

    3. Ibid., p. 74.

    4. Barbara Rogasky, *Smoke and Ashes: The Story of the Holocaust* (New York: Holiday House, 2002), pp. 75–77.

    5. Elie Wiesel, *Night* (New York: Avon Books, 1969), p. 34. Excerpts from NIGHT by Elie Wiesel, translated by Stella Rodway. Copyright © 1960 by MacGibbon & Kee. Copyright renewed © 1988 by The Collins Publishing Group. Reprinted by permission of Hill and Wang, a division of Farrar, Straus and Giroux, LLC.

    6. Ibid., p. 36.

    7. Ibid., p. 37.

    8. Raul Hilberg, *The Destruction of the European Jews*, Student Edition (New York: Holmes & Meier Publishers, Inc., 1985), p. 221.

    9. Wiesel, *Night*, p. 39.

    10. Ibid., p. 40.

    11. Ibid., p. 39.

    12. Ibid., p. 40.

    13. Ibid., p. 44.

Chapter 5. The Longest Night

1. Elie Wiesel, *Night* (New York: Avon Books, 1969), p. 56. Excerpts from NIGHT by Elie Wiesel, translated by Stella Rodway. Copyright © 1960 by MacGibbon & Kee. Copyright renewed © 1988 by The Collins Publishing Group. Reprinted by permission of Hill and Wang, a division of Farrar, Straus and Giroux, LLC.

2. Ibid., p. 66.

3. Ibid., p. 72.

4. Ibid., p. 74.

5. Ibid., p. 79.

6. "Josef Mengele," *C.A.N.D.L.E.S. Holocaust Museum*, n.d., <http://www.candles-museum.com/mengele.html> (January 26, 2005).

7. Wiesel, *Night*, p. 123.

8. Marty Moss-Coane, "Interview with Elie Wiesel," in *Elie Wiesel: Conversations*, ed. Robert Franciosi (Jackson: University Press of Mississippi, 2002), p. 168.

9. Bob Costas and Elie Wiesel, "A Wound that Will Never be Healed," in *Telling the Tale: A Tribute to Elie Wiesel*, ed. Harry James Cargas (St. Louis, Mo.: Time Being Press, 1993), p. 141.

10. Elie Wiesel, *All Rivers Run to the Sea: Memoirs* (New York: Schocken Books, Inc., 1995), p. 97. From ALL RIVERS RUN TO THE SEA by Elie Wiesel, copyright © 1995 by Elie Wiesel. Used by permission of Alfred A. Knopf, a division of Random House, Inc.

11. John S. Friedman, "The Art of Fiction LXXIX: Elie Wiesel," in *Elie Wiesel: Conversations*, ed. Robert Franciosi (Jackson: University Press of Mississippi, 2002), p. 83.

12. Wiesel, *Night*, p. 127.

Chapter 6. Wandering

1. Ted L. Estess, "A Conversation with Elie Wiesel," in *Elie Wiesel: Conversations*, ed. Robert Franciosi (Jackson: University Press of Mississippi, 2002), p. 186.

2. *First Person Singular: Elie Wiesel*, PBS DVD, Lives and Legacies Films, 2002.

3. Elie Wiesel, *All Rivers Run to the Sea: Memoirs* (New York: Schocken Books, Inc., 1995), p. 139. From ALL RIVERS RUN TO THE SEA by Elie Wiesel, copyright © 1995 by Elie Wiesel. Used by permission of Alfred A. Knopf, a division of Random House, Inc.

4. Elie Wiesel, *A Jew Today* (New York: Random House, 1978), p. 15.

5. Wiesel, *All Rivers Run to the Sea: Memoirs*, p. 178.

6. Ibid., p. 229.

7. Anson Lang, "A Conversation with Elie Wiesel," *Bold Type*, n.d., <http://www.randomhouse.com/boldtype/1299/wiesel/interview.html> (December 3, 2004).

8. Elie Wiesel, "Marginal Thoughts on Yiddish," in *Telling the Tale: A Tribute to Elie Wiesel*, ed. Harry James Cargas (St. Louis, Mo: Time Being Press, 1993), p. 35.

9. Wiesel, *A Jew Today*, p. 18.

10. "François Mauriac-Banquet Speech," June 24, 2003, <http://nobelprize.org/literature/laureates/1952/mauriac-speech.html> (December 2, 2004).

11. Wiesel, *A Jew Today*, p. 19.

Chapter 7. Storyteller

1. Paul Braunstein, "Elie Wiesel: A Lasting Tribute," in *Telling the Tale: A Tribute to Elie Wiesel*, ed. Harry James Cargas (St. Louis, Mo.: Time Being Press, 1993), p. 118.

2. Bob Costas and Elie Wiesel, "A Wound that Will Never be Healed," in *Telling the Tale: A Tribute to Elie Wiesel*, ed. Harry James Cargas (St. Louis, Mo.: Time Being Press, 1993), p. 143.

3. Elie Wiesel, *All Rivers Run to the Sea: Memoirs* (New York: Schocken Books, Inc., 1995), p. 348. From ALL RIVERS RUN TO THE SEA by Elie Wiesel, copyright © 1995 by Elie Wiesel. Used by permission of Alfred A. Knopf, a division of Random House, Inc.

4. Robert McAfee Brown, *Elie Wiesel: Messenger to All Humanity* (Notre Dame, Ind.: University of Notre Dame Press, 1983), pp. 51–108.

5. Elie Wiesel, "The America I Love," *Parade Magazine*, July 4, 2004, <http://archive.parade.com/2004/0704/0704_america.html> (December 3, 2004).

6. Elie Wiesel, *And the Sea Is Never Full: Memoirs, 1969–* (New York: Schocken Books, Inc., 1999), p. 187. From AND THE SEA IS NEVER FULL by Elie Wiesel, translated by Marion Wiesel, copyright © 1999 by Elie Wiesel. Used by permission of Alfred A. Knopf, a division of Random House, Inc.

7. Connie Bensch, "Interview with Marion Wiesel, Author of HBO Documentary that Remembers Holocaust Children," n.d., <http://

www.jewishfamily.com/culture/profiles/interview_with_marion.txt> (December 3, 2004).

8. Ibid.

9. David J. Craig, "Charles DeLisi, Marion Wiesel honored with Presidential Citizens Awards," *The B.U. Bridge*, vol. IV, no. 19, January 19, 2001, <http://www.bu.edu/bridge/archive/2001/01-19/awards.html> (December 3, 2004).

10. Brigitte-Fanny Cohen, "Talking with Elie Wiesel," in *Elie Wiesel: Conversations*, ed. Robert Franciosi (Jackson: University Press of Mississippi, 2002), p. 139.

11. Victor Malka, "Elie Wiesel: Joy and Light," in *Elie Wiesel: Conversations*, ed. Robert Franciosi (Jackson: University Press of Mississippi, 2002), p. 39.

12. Elie Wiesel, *From the Kingdom of Memory: Reminiscences* (New York: Summit, 1990), p. 21. FROM THE KINGDOM OF MEMORY: Reminiscences by Elie Wiesel. Copyright © 1990 by Elirion Associates. Used by permission of Georges Borchardt, Inc., on behalf of Elirion Associates.

13. "Conquering His Night of Despair, Wiesel Finds Day of Hope, Joy. Survivor, Chronicler of the Holocaust Shares His Faith, Fears, Frustrations," *Milwaukee Journal Sentinel*, July 1, 1997, p. 4.

14. John S. Friedman, "The Art of Fiction LXXIX: Elie Wiesel," in *Elie Wiesel: Conversations*, ed. Robert Franciosi (Jackson: University Press of Mississippi, 2002), p. 76.

15. Ibid., p. 77.

16. Anson Lang, "A Conversation with Elie Wiesel," *Bold Type*, n.d., <http://www.randomhouse.com/boldtype/1299/wiesel/interview.html> (December 3, 2004).

17. Harold Flender, "Conversation with Elie Wiesel," in *Elie Wiesel: Conversations*, ed. Robert Franciosi (Jackson: University Press of Mississippi, 2002), p. 19.

18. Wiesel, *And the Sea Is Never Full: Memoirs 1969–*, p. 122.

19. Ibid., p. 43.

20. Ibid., p. 41.

21. John S. Friedman, "The Art of Fiction LXXIX: Elie Wiesel," in *Elie Wiesel: Conversations*, ed. Robert Franciosi (Jackson: University Press of Mississippi, 2002), p. 82.

22. Samuel G. Freedman, "Bearing Witness: The Life and Work of Elie Wiesel," in *Elie Wiesel: Conversations*, ed. Robert Franciosi (Jackson: University Press of Mississippi, 2002), p. 117.

Chapter 8. Conscience

1. Elie Wiesel, *And the Sea Is Never Full: Memoirs, 1969–* (New York: Schocken Books, Inc., 1999), pp. 191–192. From AND THE SEA IS NEVER FULL by Elie Wiesel, translated by Marion Wiesel, copyright © 1999 by Elie Wiesel. Used by permission of Alfred A. Knopf, a division of Random House, Inc.

2. Treblinka was a labor camp that was turned into a death camp in 1942. In the six death camps, the numbers of victims are estimated as follows: Auschwitz 2,000,000; Belzec 600,000; Chelmno 340,000; Majdanek 1,380,000; Sobibor 250,000; and Treblinka 800,000 for a total of 5,370,000. Lucy S. Dawidowicz, *The War against the Jews 1933–1945* (New York: Holt, Rinehart & Winston, 1975), p. 135.

3. The President's Commission on the Holocaust, "Report to the President," September 27, 1979, <http://www.ushmm.org/research/library/faq/prescommprt.htm> (December 3, 2004).

4. Ibid.

5. John Silber, as quoted in "Why Elie Wiesel Can Never Forget," by Curt Schleler, *Biography Magazine*, September 1999.

6. Elie Wiesel, *From the Kingdom of Memory* (New York: Schocken Books, 1990), p. 158. FROM THE KINGDOM OF MEMORY: Reminiscences by Elie Wiesel. Copyright © 1990 by Elirion Associates. Used by permission of Georges Borchardt, Inc., on behalf of Elirion Associates.

7. Wiesel, *And the Sea Is Never Full: Memoirs, 1969–*, p. 219.

8. Jeshajahu Weinberg and Rina Elieli, *The Holocaust Museum in Washington* (New York: Rizzoli International Publications, Inc., 1995), p. 20.

9. Wiesel, *And the Sea Is Never Full: Memoirs, 1969–*, p. 222.

10. Ibid., p. 247.

11. Telephone interview with James Ingo Freed, March 26, 2004.

12. Weinberg and Elieli, *The Holocaust Museum*, p. 25.

13. Ibid.

14. Samuel G. Freedman, "Bearing Witness: The Life and Work of Elie Wiesel," *The New York Times Magazine*, October 23, 1983, p. 67.

15. Wiesel, *From the Kingdom of Memory*, p. 174.

16. Ibid., p. 176.

17. Wiesel, *And the Sea Is Never Full: Memoirs, 1969–*, p. 240.

Chapter 9. Honor

1. Elie Wiesel, *And the Sea is Never Full: Memoirs, 1969–* (New York: Schocken Books, Inc., 1999), pp. 259–260. From AND THE SEA IS NEVER FULL by Elie Wiesel, translated by Marion Wiesel, copyright © 1999 by Elie Wiesel. Used by permission of Alfred A. Knopf, a division of Random House, Inc.

2. Nobel presentation speech by Egil Aarvik, n.d., <http://nobel prize.org/peace/laureates/1986/presentation-speech.html> (December 3, 2004).

3. Wiesel, *And the Sea Is Never Full: Memoirs, 1969–*, p. 270.

4. Elie Wiesel, *From the Kingdom of Memory* (New York: Schocken Books, 1990), pp. 231–236. FROM THE KINGDOM OF MEMORY: Reminiscences by Elie Wiesel. Copyright © 1990 by Elirion Associates. Used by permission of Georges Borchardt, Inc., on behalf of Elirion Associates.

5. Wiesel, *And the Sea Is Never Full: Memoirs, 1969–*, p. 300.

6. Wiesel, *From the Kingdom of Memory*, pp. 188–189.

7. Martin Gilbert, *Never Again: A History of the Holocaust* (New York: Universe Publishing, 2000), p. 178.

8. Wiesel, *And the Sea Is Never Full: Memoirs, 1969–*, p. 395.

9. "Frequently Asked Questions . . . How many people have visited the Museum?", *United States Holocaust Memorial Museum*, March 1, 2004, <http://www.ushmm.org/research/library/faq/right_2004_03.htm#visitors> (January 26, 2005).

10. Wiesel, *And the Sea Is Never Full: Memoirs, 1969–*, p. 249.

11. Ibid., p. 337.

12. Elie Wiesel, *Curriculum Vitae*, 2004.

Chapter 10. *Gadol b'Israel* (A Great Man of Israel)

1. Alan L. Berger, "Review of The Judges," *Shofar: An Interdisciplinary Journal of Jewish Studies*, Spring 2003, vol. 21, issue 3, pp. 151–153.

2. Curt Schleler, "Why Elie Wiesel Can Never Forget," *Biography Magazine*, September 1999, p. 69.

3. Ibid.

4. Edward B. Fiske, "Elie Wiesel: Archivist with a Mission," in *Elie Wiesel: Conversations*, ed. Robert Franciosi (Jackson: University Press of Mississippi, 2002), p. 43.

5. Leo Eitenger, "To Bring Hope and Help," in *Telling the Tale: A Tribute to Elie Wiesel*, ed. Harry James Cargas (St. Louis, Mo.: Time Being Press, 1993), p. 95.

6. Edward Fiske, "Archivist," p. 41.

7. Samuel G. Freedman, "Bearing Witness: The Life and Work of Elie Wiesel," in *Elie Wiesel: Conversations*, ed. Robert Franciosi (Jackson: University Press of Mississippi, 2002), p. 110.

8. Alan Dershowitz, "A Biblical Life," *Elie Wiesel: First Person Singular*, 1997, <http://www.pbs.org/eliewiesel/life/dershowitz.html> (December 3, 2004).

9. Robert McAfee Brown, *Elie Wiesel: Messenger to All Humanity* (Notre Dame, Ind.: University of Notre Dame Press, 1983), pp. 217–218.

10. Henry James Cargas in "Night As Autobiography," in *Telling the Tale: A Tribute to Elie Wiesel*, ed. Harry James Cargas (St. Louis, Mo.: Time Being Press, 1993), pp. 107–108.

11. "Secretary-General Praises Elie Wiesel on 75th Birthday as a Good Friend, Staunch Defender of Victims of Hatred, Bigotry," *United Nations Information Service*, May 26, 2004, <http://www.unis.unvienna.org/unis/pressrels/2004/sgsm9326.html> (December 3, 2004).

12. "Elie Wiesel Interview," *Academy of Achievement*, June 29, 1996, <http://www.achievement.org/autodoc/page/wie0int-1> (December 3, 2004).

13. Elie Wiesel, *And the Sea is Never Full: Memoirs, 1969–* (New York: Schocken Books, Inc., 1999), p. 410. From AND THE SEA IS NEVER FULL by Elie Wiesel, translated by Marion Wiesel, copyright © 1999 by Elie Wiesel. Used by permission of Alfred A. Knopf, a division of Random House, Inc.

14. An interview with Kerry Kennedy Cuomo, *Speak Truth to Power*, n.d., <http://www.pbs.org/speaktruthtopower/elie> (December 3, 2004).

15. Elie Wiesel and Richard D. Heffner, *Conversations with Elie Wiesel* (New York: Schocken Books, 2001), p. 14.

16. Elie Wiesel in "The Perils of Indifference: Lessons Learned from a Violent Century," a speech given in the East Room of the White House on April 12, 1999, hosted by President Bill and First Lady Hillary Rodham Clinton. The entire speech is available in transcript and for listening at <http://clinton4.nara.gov/textonly/WH/New/html/1990413-850.html> (December 3, 2004).

Glossary

anti-Semitism—Having or showing prejudice against, discrimination against, or even persecution of Jews.

Aryan—A hypothetical prehistoric Indo-European language, the parent of many modern European languages. Nazis used the term to refer to northern Europeans who are tall, blond, and blue eyed, but ethnologically, there is no Aryan race.

block—A barrack that housed prisoners in Nazi concentration camps.

Cabala (or Kabbala)—The study or practice of Jewish mystical sciences.

cantata—A musical composition that tells a story, sung but not acted.

concentration camp—A labor or death camp where Nazis sent people they considered dangerous to their ideals. "Concentrated" in the camps, prisoners were worked to death, tortured, or killed.

crematory—A furnace for burning dead bodies.

death camp—The six camps where Jews and other victims of the Nazis were murdered.

de-Judaize—To remove the idea of "Jewishness" from an event or text.

deport—To force a person to leave a country by official government orders.

Diaspora—The dispersion of Jews all over the world.

dictator—A ruler with absolute power.

gallows—An upright frame with a crossbeam and a rope, used for hanging condemned prisoners.

gentile—A non-Jewish person.

Gestapo—The secret police force of the SS in the German Nazi state.

ghetto—A small isolated area in a city in which Jews were forced to live during World War II.

Hasid—Literally "pious man." A disciple of the movement founded by the Baal Shem Tov and influenced by the Cabala.

Kaddish—The Jewish prayer for the dead.

kapo—A prisoner who worked for the Nazis as a block or barracks leader.

kosher food—Food prepared according to strict Jewish dietary laws.

Mein Kampf—Hitler's book that details his plans to make Germany the ruler of the world.

memoir—An autobiography that is anecdotal and introspective rather than purely factual and chronological.

mysticism—A belief in the possibility of attaining knowledge through meditation and contemplation.

Nazi—The abbreviation for *Nationalsozialistische Deutsche Arbeiterpartei*, translated as the National Socialist German Workers' Party. The Nazi party was the only political party allowed in Germany from 1933 to 1945.

Nobel Prize—Annual international prizes given by the Nobel Foundation in Norway for distinction in physics, chemistry, economics, medicine, literature, and the promotion of peace.

Nuremberg Trials—Postwar trials of Nazi war criminals, held in Nuremberg, Germany, beginning in October 1945.

Palestine—A region in the Middle East comprising parts of modern Israel and Jordan, also known as "the Holy Land."

rabbi (or rebbe)—A scholar and teacher of Jewish law and history.

refugee—A person who flees a country to seek safety elsewhere.

selection—The Nazi's process of choosing which prisoners would live and which ones would be killed in the death camps.

shtetl—A small, often isolated, Jewish village in Eastern Europe.

SS—The abbreviation for *Schutzstaffel*, meaning Elite Guard. The SS began as Hitler's bodyguards and then became the unit that ran the concentration camps.

synagogue—A Jewish house of prayer, religious ceremony, and community.

Talmud—The collection of Jewish oral law, commentaries, and teachings.

testimony—A statement or declaration, often given under oath, that describes an historical event.

Third Reich—Hitler's empire, intended to last a thousand years, it lasted from 1933 to 1945.

Torah—Specifically, the five books of Moses in the Bible. More generally, the sum total of Jewish law and learning.

Vichy—A city in central France that was the seat of the French government that collaborated with the Nazis after France's occupation in 1940.

Further Reading

Books by Elie Wiesel

Wiesel, Elie. *After the Darkness: Reflections on the Holocaust.* New York: Schocken Books, 2002.

_____. *Against Silence: The Voice and Vision of Elie Wiesel*, ed. Irving Abrahamson. New York: Schocken Books, 1988.

_____. *All Rivers Run to the Sea: Memoirs.* New York: Schocken Books, Inc., 1995.

_____. *And the Sea is Never Full: Memoirs, 1969–.* New York: Schocken Books, Inc., 1999.

_____, and Michaël de Saint Cheron. *Evil and Exile*, 2nd ed., trans. Jon Rothschild and Jody Gladding. Notre Dame, Ind.: University of Notre Dame Press, 2000.

_____. *Five Biblical Portraits.* Notre Dame, Ind.: University of Notre Dame Press, 1981.

_____. *Four Hasidic Masters and their Struggle Against Melancholy.* Notre Dame, Ind.: University of Notre Dame Press, 1978.

_____. *From the Kingdom of Memory.* New York: Schocken Books, 1990.

_____. *A Jew Today*, trans. Marion Wiesel. New York: Vintage Books, 1979.

_____. *The Jews of Silence*, trans. Neal Kozodoy. New York: Schocken Books, 1987.

_____, and John Cardinal O'Connor. *A Journey of Faith.* New York: Donald I. Fine, 1990.

_____. *Legends of Our Time.* New York: Schocken Books, 2004.

_____. *Messengers of God: Biblical Portraits and Legends*, trans. Marion Wiesel. New York: Summit Books, 1985.

_____. *Night.* New York: Avon Books, 1960.

_____. *One Generation After.* New York: Random House, 1965.

_____. *Paroles d'étranger: Textes, Contes et Dialogues.* Paris: Editions du Seuil, 1982.

_____. *A Passover Haggadah: As Commented Upon by Elie Wiesel and Illustrated by Mark Podwal.* Simon & Schuster, 1993.

_____. *Sages and Dreamers: Biblical, Talmudic, and Hasidic Portraits and Legends.* New York: Summit Books, 1991.

_____. *Signes d'exode: Essais, Histoires, Dialogues.* Paris: B. Grasset, 1985.

_____, and Albert H. Friedlander. *The Six Days of Destruction: Meditations Towards Hope.* New York: Pergamon Press, 1988.

_____. *Somewhere a Master: Hasidic Portraits and Legends.* New York: Schocken Books, 2005.

_____. *Souls on Fire: Portraits and Legends of Hasidic Masters,* trans. Marion Wiesel. Northvale, N.J.: Jason Aronson, 1993.

_____. *Wise Men and Their Tales.* New York: Schocken Books, 2003.

Books on Elie Wiesel

Bloom, Harold, ed. *Modern Critical Interpretations: Elie Wiesel's Night.* Langhorne, Pa.: Chelsea House Publishers, 2001.

Cargas, Harry James, ed. *Telling the Tale: A Tribute to Elie Wiesel.* St. Louis, Mo.: Time Being Press, 1993.

Franciosi, Robert, ed. *Elie Wiesel: Conversations.* Jackson: University Press of Mississippi, 2002.

Rosen, Alan, ed. *Celebrating Elie Wiesel: Stories, Essays, Reflections.* Notre Dame, Ind.: University of Notre Dame Press, 1998.

Sibleman, Simon P. *Silence in the Novels of Elie Wiesel.* New York: St. Martin's Press, 1995.

Books on the Holocaust

Gilbert, Martin. *A History of the Twentieth Century, Volume I: 1900–1933.* New York: William Morrow & Co., Inc., 1997.

_____. *A History of the Twentieth Century, Volume II: 1933–1959.* New York: HarperCollins, 2000.

_____. *Never Again: A History of the Holocaust.* New York: Universe Publishing, 2000.

Hilberg, Raul. *The Destruction of the European Jews,* Student Edition. New York: Holmes & Meier Publishers, Inc., 1985.

Isaacson, Judith Magyar. *Seed of Sarah.* Champaign, Ill.: University of Illinois Press, 1991.

Lengyel, Olga. *Five Chimneys.* Chicago, Ill.: Academy Chicago Publishers, 1995.

Levi, Primo. *Survival in Auschwitz.* New York: Simon & Schuster, 1995.

Rogasky, Barbara. *Smoke and Ashes: The Story of the Holocaust.* New York: Holiday House, Inc., 2002.

Weinberg, Jeshajahu and Rina Elieli. *The Holocaust Museum in Washington.* New York: Rizzoli International Publications, Inc., 1995.

Wiesel, Marion, ed. *To Give Them Light: The Legacy of Roman Vishniac.* New York: Simon and Schuster, 1993.

Books on Other Holocaust Survivors

Ben-Zvi, Hava. *Eva's Journey: A Young Girl's True Story.* iUniverse, 2004.

Bitton-Jackson, Livia. *Hello, America.* New York: Simon & Schuster Books for Young Readers, 2004.

Brostoff, Anita, ed., with Sheila Chamovitz, ed. *Flares of Memory: Stories of Childhood During the Holocaust.* Oxford University Press, 2002.

Hollander, Eugene. *From the Hell of the Holocaust: A Survivor's Story.* Katv Publishers, Inc., 2001.

Landau, Elaine. *We Survived the Holocaust.* Franklin Watts, 1991.

Levine, Karen. *Hana's Suitcase: A True Story.* Morton Grove, Ill.: Albert Whitman, 2003.

McCann, Michelle R. Luba: *The Angel of Bergen-Belsen.* As told by Luba Tryszynska-Frederick. Berkeley, Calif.: Tricycle Press, 2003.

Shuter, Jane. *Survivors of the Holocaust.* Chicago, Ill.: Heinemann Library, 2003.

Soumerai, Eve Nussbaum and Carol D. Schulz. *A Voice From the Holocaust.* Westport, Conn.: Greenwood Press, 2003.

Zee, Ruth Vander. *Erika's Story.* Mankato, Minn.: Creative Editions, 2003.

Internet Addresses

Elie Wiesel: First Person Singular
<http://www.pbs.org/>

*In the "Explore by Topic" drop-down box
in the upper-right corner, select "History."
Under the "Topic Index" sub-heading at the
right, click on "Biographies." Scroll down
and click on "Elie Wiesel" at the left.*

The Elie Wiesel Foundation for Humanity
<http://www.eliewieselfoundation.org>

United States Holocaust Memorial Museum
<http://www.ushmm.org>

Index